Macraweave

Macramé meets weaving with
18 stunning home decor projects

AMY MULLINS &
MARNIA RYAN-RAISON

DAVID & CHARLES

www.davidandcharles.com

Contents

Introduction

This book is your must-have guide to macraweaving, the exciting new craft that brings together two timelessly popular fibre arts, macramé and weaving. By combining the essential knots of macramé with three of the most fundamental weaving techniques, you will discover how simple it can be to work with texture and colour to make beautiful, eye-catching pieces for your home.

Whether you are looking to learn a fresh skill, or to take your macramé to a whole new level, you'll find everything you need right here. We've put together an enticing selection of eighteen projects for you to choose from to satisfy all your creative ambitions, whether you are searching for functionality or for an artistic feature to transform a room.

Every project, be it our simple starter Keeper Key Rings to our phenomenal Pride and Joy Wall Hanging, is explained in clear step-by-step detail. We begin with the macramé element for each, as this must be done first to create a structure of negative spaces, or warp threads, through which the weft threads are woven in the weaving element. In devising our designs, we have aimed to introduce you to a wide variety of decorative possibilities, using an assortment of rope in different fibres and thicknesses, exploring rich colourways and interesting textural techniques.

You'll find more information on the materials we have used in the Techniques section, along with essential illustrated reference on the knots and the weaves, as well as a comprehensive guide to understanding the macraweave technique, which we suggest you practise in full before beginning your first project. Each project chapter lists the materials you will need and the techniques required, so you can review the tying and weaving sequences as you go; follow these precisely and you will find that even the most complex of designs is easier to achieve than you may have expected.

Techniques

Understanding Macraweave

A macraweave is a fusion of the textile-making arts of macramé and weaving, but to understand the macraweave, we must first take a look at macramé and its negative spaces.

The negative spaces in a macramé piece are the areas where there are no knots tied. The vertical cords of these negative spaces resemble that of the warp threads in weaving and can therefore be used in the same way.

A macraweave is made by first making a macramé structure with a negative space or spaces, then applying weaving techniques through the negative space of the macramé. The tension of the negative space is very important as there is no device (such as a loom) to facilitate the weave, so you must make sure that all the vertical cords in the negative space are uniformly taut before attempting to weave through them.

Once you have created a negative space (the warp) you will begin to weave in new threads horizontally using weaving techniques. These cords can be referred to as the weft and it is also important to keep a uniform tension with these cords.

negative space
(the warp)

The macramé structure is the first stage of creating a macraweave piece. The vertical cords where no macramé knots are tied, that is the negative space, act as the warp. It is important to keep these cords uniformly taut so your weaving is neat.

Note: Each project features a photo or photos annotated with circled numbers that cross reference to the step-by-step instructions. However, due to the nature of creating the piece, some steps can't be shown, e.g., mounting techniques, or where macramé cords have been woven over, or where rya knot fringing (Pride and Joy Wall Hanging) or project construction (shoulder bag and clutch purse) obscures steps. Take the time to read the pattern instructions carefully before you begin.

Essential Terminology

Before you start on your macraweave journey, there is some essential terminology that you need to familiarise yourself with. This list covers all of the terms used for the macramé knotting and weaving techniques:

Negative space: The area where there are no knots tied in a macramé piece. The negative space is used as the warp threads in a macraweave.

Warp: The vertical yarns that are held stationary and through which the weft threads are woven. In a macraweave, the warp will comprise pre-existing macramé threads rather than the cords that are attached to the loom in traditional weaving.

Weft: The yarn or set of yarns that are worked through the warp threads in a horizontal manner

Sinnet: A vertical column of tied knots.

Row: A series of knots tied side by side.

Working cords: The cords that are used to create the knot.

Filler cords: The non–working cords around which the working cords are tied.

Holding cord: The object onto which cords are tied, that is a ring, a dowel or another piece of rope.

Alternate cords: The means by which you create a new knot by taking half of the cords from a previous knot together with half of the cords from its adjacent knot to form a new group.

the weft

Once the macramé element is complete, the weaving element can begin. Here the peach rope is the weft and it has been woven through the negative space using a simple tabby weave in a two over two under pattern.

Materials

This section gives us the opportunity to introduce you to the most important material of all for any macraweave artist, the cords for tying the knots and weaving the negative spaces, as well as a few basic tools that you will need. The exact materials used for each design are listed at the beginning of each project chapter.

For the macramé structure in the projects we have used either thick cotton rope or hemp. When choosing your cotton rope, note that we have used a very soft 3-ply twisted cotton, although this can be substituted for cotton string. For the weaving element we have used a number of different fibre types, from soft yarns such as tapestry wool and cotton thread, to more textured materials including hemp, jute and sisal.

The length and thickness of the cords required for each design is given in the materials list at the start of each project. We suggest that you use the exact materials as we have for the macramé structure, but when you are confident with the macraweave technique, do explore making substitutions for our choices for the weaving element. Cord is available through the authors' website **www.edeneve.com.au** or from all good suppliers and haberdashery stores.

Tools

The basic tools you will need are scissors and a tape measure. Some of the projects do require the use of a hot glue gun and if so, this is noted in the materials list at the beginning of the project chapter. Unlike traditional loom weaving, the weaving element in our macraweave projects rarely requires tools. We have hand woven almost all of the projects, however some of the smaller more intricate projects, such as the key ring, benefit from the use of a yarn or tapestry needle. This type of needle has a rounded tip, with a large eye for threading thicker threads through. It is also helpful for weaving in the cord ends for a neat finish.

Note: When buying and cutting rope and cord, use either the metric or the imperial measurements given – do not switch between the two.

General Techniques

Before you begin working on a piece, it is important to familiarise yourself with all the techniques you may require to create your chosen project. Start by taking the time to read through this section, which includes handy tips on getting started as well as advice on how to neatly finish your macraweave masterpieces.

Mounting Techniques

It is very important to have a firm tension when working on the macramé structure and weaving element of your projects, so set yourself up with the correct equipment to mount your projects.

For small projects such as the jewellery and key rings, we recommend investing in a project board. This is printed with a grid and cords, and hardware can be attached to it using T-pins. Alternatively, a flat surface and adhesive tape will suffice.

For most of the projects, we have used a clothes rack as a work station. You can use S-hooks to secure a ring or a piece of dowel to the rack. Alternatively, you can simply use rope to tie them on to your rack.

Wrapping a Ring

Secure one end of your rope length onto the ring with craft glue or a hot glue gun, pressing it down firmly. Taking the long end of the cord through the ring, wrap the rope around the ring to cover it completely leaving just enough space to secure the cord end to the ring, again with glue, once trimmed.

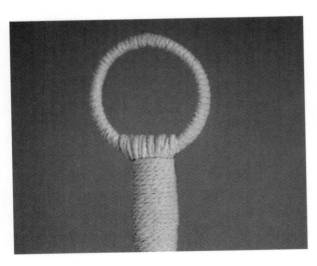

Fraying

This is a finishing technique where the rope is unravelled by separating each strand into its constituent parts to create a fringe, or for a tassel.

Plaiting

Plaiting is the interlacing of three cords or groups of cords to create a braid. Cross the left-hand cord over the centre cord to become the centre cord. Then cross the right-hand cord over the new centre cord so that it now takes the centre position. Continue to alternate left- and right-hand cords to the centre position to form the braid.

Numbering Cords

This is a way of counting cords to find the exact section to begin working from in a macramé pattern. Cords are counted from left to right, usually mentally for smaller projects where fewer cords are used. When working on large projects that use many cords to create the pattern, it is easy to lose count. To help you to keep track, you can temporarily tie a piece of bright yarn around every tenth cord, or you can use pegs to keep groups of cords together.

Joining Weaving Cords

To create a thicker textured yarn, lay cord ends of equal lengths together and use tape to secure them.

Adding Weaving Cords

This technique enables you to add more yarn if you have run out or if you want to change the type of yarn you are weaving with. Simply add in the new thread next to the previously worked thread, keeping the over and under pattern.

Weaving Finishing Technique

For Macramé Knots

Bring the cord ends to the back of the design and pass them underneath the loop of one or more knots.

For Weft Threads

Bring loose weft ends at the side or the front of the woven area to the back. Use a needle or your hands to weave in all ends, so they can't be seen at the front.

Lacing Up

The sides of the pocket on the clutch purse are laced together by threading the holding cord through the spaces in the alternating square knot patterns.

Whip Stitch

This is a basic stitch that is used to secure two layers of material together. Be sure to work through both layers and aim to keep your stitches uniform.

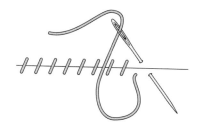

The Knots

Overhand Knot

An overhand knot is a way of tying a single cord to stop the end from fraying.

1. Bring the cord end up and over itself to form a loop.

2. Pull the cord end through the loop to secure.

Note: To make a **_double overhand_** or **_triple overhand_** knot, simply repeat the steps as necessary.

Wrapped Knot

A wrapped knot is generally used at the top and bottom of a hanging piece to secure the cords together.

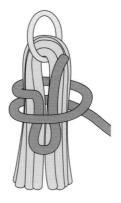

1. Form a loop just below the cords to be wrapped, with the short end facing upwards.

2. Bring the long end back up to just below the short end and wrap firmly around all of the cords. Wrap until it reaches your desired length, ensuring that you do not cover the loop. Bring the long end down through the loop.

3. Pull the short end up until the loop is about half way through the wrap. Trim the ends of the cords used to make the wrapped knot.

Half Hitch Knots

Half hitch knots are important and widely used in macramé. They are made with a working cord and holding cord, and can be used in a vertical, horizontal or diagonal manner by changing the angle of the holding cord. These instructions show you how to create various half hitch knots.

1. Begin with the working cord 2 under the holding cord 1. Bring the working cord up and over the holding cord and down through the loop. This is a **half hitch**.

2. Bring the working cord up and over the holding cord again, completing the **double half hitch**.

3. Bring the working cord up and over the holding cord a third time to create a **triple half hitch**.

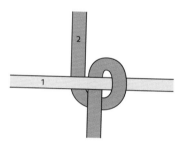

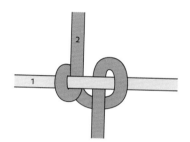

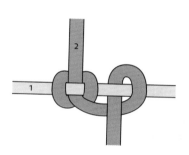

Horizontal Double Half Hitch

This is a series of double half hitches tied along a horizontal holding cord.

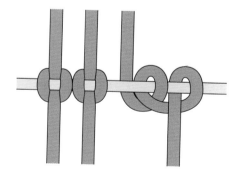

Diagonal Double Half Hitch

This is a series of double half hitches tied along a diagonal holding cord.

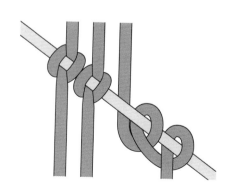

Reverse Lark's Head Knot

The reverse lark's head knot is most commonly used as a way of mounting cords onto a piece of dowel or another horizontal holding cord.

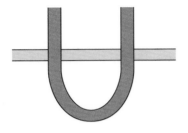 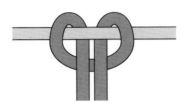

1. Fold one length of cord in half and place it over the holding cord or dowel.

2. Bring the cord ends through the loop.

3. Pull the cord ends to secure the knot.

Double Reverse Lark's Head Knot

A double reverse lark's head knot is a handy knot to start with when you want to finish with double half hitches, as it ensures the width will be kept the same.

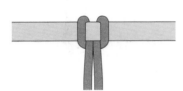 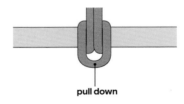

pull down

1. Tie a reverse lark's head knot onto the holding cord or dowel.

2. Bring the cord ends upwards and the loop down.

3. Continue to loop the cord ends around the holding cord or dowel.

4. Bring the cord ends through the loop so they are sitting over it.

Square Knot

The square knot is one of the most commonly used macramé knots. Variations of the square knot can be achieved by using different numbers of filler cords and working cords. However, a standard square knot only uses four cords (as the diagrams shown). The basic square knot can be used to create lots of different patterns.

1. Number cords 1 to 4. The outside cords 1 and 4 are the working cords and cords 2 and 3 are the filler cords. Bring cord 1 over the filler cords and under cord 4.

2. Now bring cord 4 under the filler cords and back up between cords 1 and 2 to lay over cord 1.

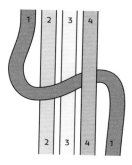

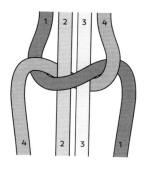

3. Bring cord 1 back over the filler cords and under cord 4.

4. Now bring cord 4 under the filler cords and back up between cords 3 and 1, and pull the working cords to tighten the knot.

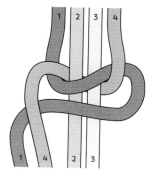

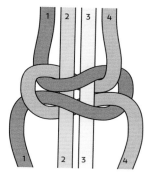

Alternating Square Knot Pattern

The alternating square knot pattern is one of the most commonly used in macramé.

1. Tie square knots in a horizontal row (see Square Knot); for the purpose of this diagram two have been used, however this technique can be used with more square knots.

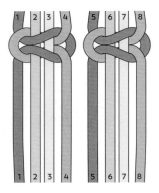

2. Alternate cords, bringing together cords 3 and 4 with cords 5 and 6, to create a square knot on a new row, using cords 3 and 6 as the working cords and cords 4 and 5 as the filler cords.

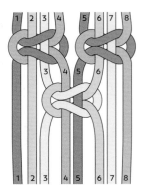

3. For the next row, tie two square knots as in step 1, with cords 1–4 for the first square knot and cords 5–8 for the second square knot.

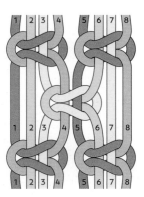

Decreasing Square Knot Pattern

With this pattern, the amount of square knots tied in each consecutive row decreases. For the diagrams as shown, the decreasing square knot pattern has been worked using twelve cords (beginning with three square knots); however, fewer or more cords may be used (this will be referred to in the individual pattern).

1. Tie a row of square knots (see Square Knot) with cords 1–4, 5–8 and 9–12.

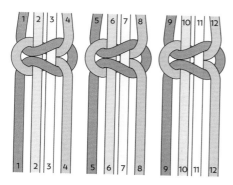

2. Tie the second row of square knots with cords 3–6 and 7–10.

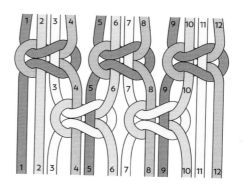

3. Tie the third row of square knots with cords 5–8.

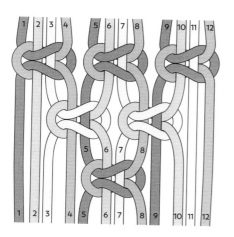

Square Knot Button

The square knot button, a decorative feature seen on the collar necklace, is made by tying a sequence of three square knots, then running the filler cords through the middle gap above them to create a rounded button shape.

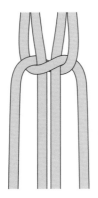

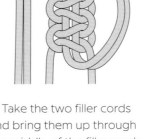

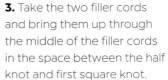

1. First start by tying a half knot (see Half Knot).

2. Now drop down approximately 1cm (⅜in), or just enough space for two cords to fit through, and tie three square knots directly beneath one another.

3. Take the two filler cords and bring them up through the middle of the filler cords in the space between the half knot and first square knot.

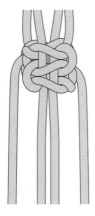

4. Continue to bring the filler cords back down. You will now have a square knot button.

5. Secure the square knot button in place by tying a single square knot beneath it (see diagram) and pull it tight so that it 'disappears' beneath the square knot button.

Adding Cords with Square Knot

Macramé cords are sometimes required to be added to existing cords during the process by adding a single cord to either the existing filler cords or the working cords of a square knot (as instructed in the pattern) to create another square knot.

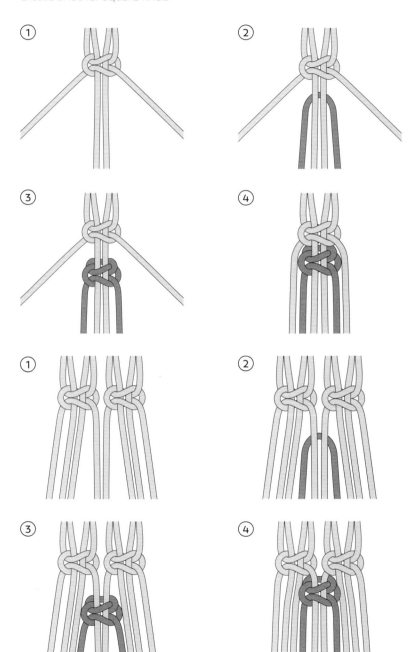

To filler cords

1. Place the working cords of the existing knot to the side.

2. Take the cord to be added and fold it in half. Place the centre fold of this cord so that it is sitting behind the filler cords to give you four cords hanging down.

3. Continue to tie a square knot as you normally would.

4. Push up the square knot you have made so it is sitting directly beneath the existing one.

To working cords

1. Bring together a working cord of one square knot with a working cord from its adjacent square knot.

2. Take the cord to be added and fold it in half. Place the centre fold of this cord so it is sitting behind the existing two working cords to give you four cords hanging down.

3. Continue to tie a square knot as you normally would.

4. Push up the square knot you have made so it is sitting directly beneath and in the middle of the two existing ones.

Half Knot

A half knot is basically half a square knot. Half knots can be tied in rows and worked to create an alternating pattern, too.

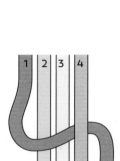

1. Number cords 1 to 4. The outside cords 1 and 4 are the working cords and cords 2 and 3 are the filler cords. Bring cord 1 over the filler cords and under cord 4.

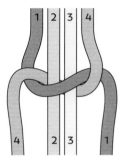

2. Now bring cord 4 under the filler cords and back up between cords 1 and 2 to lay over cord 1.

Half knots can be worked in an ***alternating half knot pattern*** in the same way that square knots can be worked in an alternating square knot pattern (see Square Knots: Alternating Square Knot Pattern). The pocket of the handy clutch purse project is made with an alternating half knot pattern.

Chinese Crown Knot

To tie the Chinese crown knot at the centre of the coaster and the placemat projects, work on a flat surface. The single cords shown in the diagrams and photo sample represent cord groups of several cords.

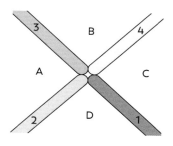

1. Take one cord group and place it on top of the other cord group so they cross over at the centre. Number the cord group ends 1 to 4 and label the spaces in between the cord groups A to D.

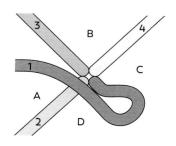

2. Place cord group end 1 into space A, ensuring that there is a loop at the fold.

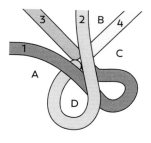

3. Place cord group end 2 over cord group end 1 and into space B. Bring cord group end 2 all the way into the centre and do not leave a loop (see step 4).

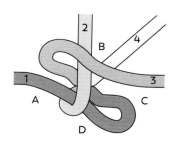

4. Place cord group end 3 over cord group ends 2 and 4 and into space C.

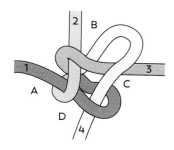

5. Place cord group end 4 through the loop made in step 2 bringing it into space D.

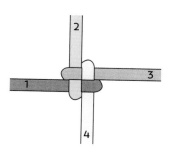

6. Pull all cord group ends together evenly until the knot is formed.

The Weaves

Rya Knots

Although rya knots can be used anywhere, they are most often used for fringing at the base of a piece to create length. When cut short, they give a shaggy rug or pompom-like effect as on the Pride & Joy wall hanging.

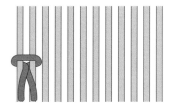

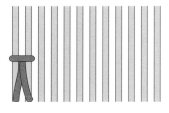

1. Fold the length of cord in half. Place the folded edge over the first and second warp cords, bringing the cord ends through to the back.

2. Take the cord ends through the middle of warp cords 1 and 2.

3. Pull the cord ends to secure the knot in place.

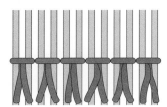

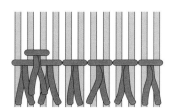

4. Make additional rya knots every two warp threads to create a row of rya knots. Cords can be kept long for fringing or cut short to create a 'shaggy rug' look.

5. When creating rows of rya knots, you can alternate the warp cords. Simply place a rya knot on the adjacent warps from each of the two rya knots below it.

Tabby Weave

A tabby weave is the most common and simplest form of weaving. It is made when the weft threads pass over and under continuously through the warp.

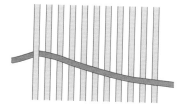

1. Bring your weft thread under the first warp thread allowing for thread tail of at least 10–15cm (4–6in) or as directed in the pattern instruction.

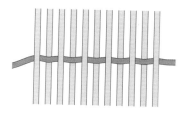

2. Weave your weft thread over the second warp thread, and continue to weave under, over, under, over until the row is completed.

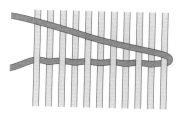

3. To continue with another row, bring your weft thread upwards ready to start weaving back along the warp threads.

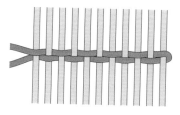

4. Continue to weave under, over, under, over until the row is completed. Note that the weft threads should be sitting in the opposite way from the first row. So, if a weft thread is over the warp in the first row, it will be sitting under the warp in the second row.

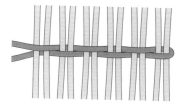

5. The tabby weave can be used with different combinations of the under and over pattern. Here is an example of a two under and two over pattern.

When the same size material is used for the warp and the weft, the tabby weave creates a chequerboard effect and is referred to as a 'balanced' weave. When different sizes of material are used for the warp and the weft, the weft can conceal the warp and produce a raised or overlapping effect.

Soumak Weave

The soumak weave brings a dimensional look to a piece because the weft threads are wrapped around the warp. When more than one row is woven, it creates a beautiful braid feature.

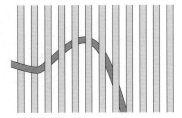

1. Bring the weft thread over the first two warp threads allowing for a thread tail of at least 10–15cm (4–6in) or as directed in the pattern instruction.

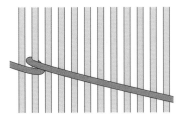

2. Loop the weft thread around the second warp thread by bringing it under and over it.

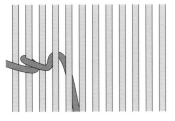

3. Bring the weft thread over the third warp thread.

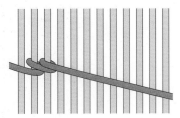

4. Loop the weft thread around the third warp thread by bringing it under and over it.

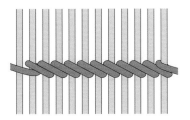

5. Continue looping the weft thread around all the warp threads until the row is complete.

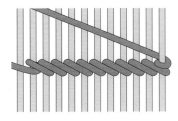

6. To complete another row, bring your weft thread up and under the last warp thread.

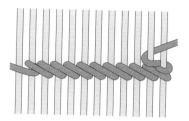

7. Bring the weft thread over and under the second from last warp thread.

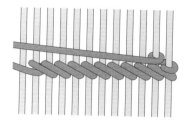

8. Loop it around the second from last warp thread by bringing it back over. It will now be facing towards the left, ready to continue the soumak pattern in the other direction.

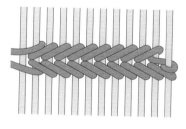

9. Continue to loop the weft thread around the warp threads to create a braided effect.

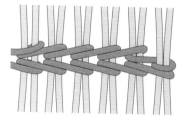

10. The soumak weave can be used with different combinations of the under and over pattern. Here is an example of a two under and over pattern.

Projects

———

Keeper Key Rings

If you are looking for a stylish way to keep your keys safe but distinctly yours, we have two different variations on our key ring design. Not only are these a great way to identify your keys from your partner's or flatmate's, they make great starter projects incorporating a basic square knot macramé pattern with two fundamental weaving techniques to have you macraweaving before you know it.

Materials

Quantities given are for each key ring

- 6.9m (22½ft) of 2mm (³⁄₃₂in) natural cotton rope
- Swivel clasp key ring with an area of 3cm (1⅛in) to mount rope
- 1.5m (5ft) each of tapestry wool in two different colours
- Tapestry needle with blunt tip
- Five beads with bead hole of 4mm (⁵⁄₃₂in) (for key ring with beads)

Techniques

For both key rings

- Reverse Lark's Head Knot
- Horizontal Double Half Hitch
- Tabby Weave
- Overhand Knot
- Fraying
- Weaving Finishing Technique

For woven key ring

- Alternating Square Knot Pattern
- Adding Weaving Cords

For key ring with beads

- Square Knot
- Soumak Weave

Preparation

Quantities given are for each key ring

- Cut 6 x 1m (3¼ft) lengths of 2mm (³⁄₃₂in) natural cotton rope
- Cut 3 x 30cm (12in) lengths of 2mm (³⁄₃₂in) natural cotton rope
- Cut 1 x 1.5m (5ft) of colour 1 tapestry wool
- Cut 1 x 1.5m (5ft) of colour 2 tapestry wool

Macramé Element for
Woven Key Ring

1. Secure the key ring to a project board using a T-pin and mount the six 1m (3¼ft) lengths of rope onto the key ring using reverse lark's head knots.

2. Directly beneath the reverse lark's head knots, begin the first panel of alternating square knot pattern starting by tying a row of three square knots.

3. Alternate cords (see Essential Terminology) and tie a row of two square knots.

4. Alternate cords and tie a row of three square knots.

5. Place a 30cm (12in) length of rope horizontally directly beneath the last row of knots. This is now the holding cord (see Essential Terminology).

6. Tie horizontal double half hitches with all cords along the holding cord.

7. Drop down 3cm (1⅛in) and place another 30cm (12in) length of rope horizontally to become a holding cord.

8. Tie horizontal double half hitches with all cords along the holding cord. This creates a negative space that will be used as the warp for your weave in steps 15 and 16.

9. Continue with the second panel of alternating square knot pattern, starting by tying a row of three square knots.

10. Alternate cords and tie a row of two square knots

11. Alternate cords and tie a row of three square knots.

12. Place a 30cm (12in) length of rope horizontally directly beneath the last row of knots. This is now the holding cord

13. Tie horizontal double half hitches with all cords along the holding cord

14. Trim cord ends to your desired length and tie an overhand knot at the bottom of each cord. Fray the cord ends as desired.

Weaving Element for
Woven Key Ring

15. Thread the tapestry needle with colour 1 tapestry wool (to be used as your weft thread) and, starting from the base of the negative space, tabby weave through the negative space for 1.5cm (⅝in).

16. Add colour 2 tapestry wool and tabby weave through the negative space for 1.5cm (⅝in) or until completely woven.

17. Use a weaving finishing technique to weave in cord ends through the back of the design.

Macramé Element for
Key Ring with Beads

1. Secure the key ring to a project board using a T-pin and mount the six 1m (3¼ft) lengths of rope onto the key ring using reverse lark's head knots.

2. Directly beneath the reverse lark's head knots, tie a row of three square knots.

3. Thread a bead onto cords 2 and 3, cords 4 and 5, cords 6 and 7, cords 8 and 9, and cords 10 and 11.

4. Tie a row of three square knots directly beneath the beads.

5. Place a 30cm (12in) length of rope horizontally directly beneath the last row of knots. This is now the holding cord (see Essential Terminology).

6. Tie horizontal double half hitches with all cords along the holding cord.

7. Drop down 2cm (¾in) and place another 30cm (12in) length of rope horizontally to become a holding cord.

8. Tie horizontal double half hitches with all cords along the holding cord. This creates negative space 1 that will be used as the warp for your weave in steps 12 and 13.

9. Drop down 3cm (1⅛in) and place another 30cm (12in) length of rope horizontally to become a holding cord. This creates negative space 2 that will be used as the warp for your weave in steps 12 and 13.

10. Tie horizontal double half hitches with all cords along the holding cord.

11. Trim cord ends to your desired length and tie an overhand knot at the bottom of each cord. Fray the cord ends as desired.

Weaving Element for Key Ring with Beads

12. Thread the tapestry needle with colour 1 tapestry wool (to be used as your weft thread) and soumak weave through negative space 1 for 1.5cm (⅝in) or until completely woven.

13. Thread the tapestry needle with colour 2 tapestry wool and tabby weave through negative space 2 for 2cm (¾in) or until completely woven.

14. Use a weaving finishing technique to weave in cord ends through the back of the design.

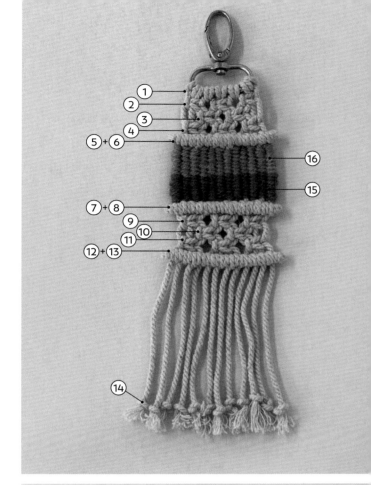

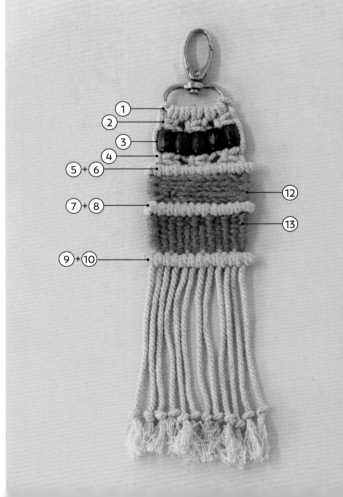

Vamp It Up
Cushion Cover

Turn a plain linen cushion into a statement piece with this beautiful macraweave panel. Incorporating half knot and square knot sections, it is a great way to refresh your macramé skills, while trying your hand at small sections of weaving patterns. Finished off with long fringing, this accessory will add a touch of class to your home.

Materials

- 80.4m (262ft) of 5mm (³⁄₁₆in) natural cotton rope
- 4m (13¼ft) each of 5mm (³⁄₁₆in) cotton rope in two different colours of your choosing
- 40 x 40cm (16 x 16in) cushion cover and insert
- Hot glue gun (optional)

Techniques

- Horizontal Double Half Hitch
- Half Knot
- Alternating Half Knot Pattern
- Square Knot
- Overhand Knot
- Soumak Weave
- Tabby Weave
- Weaving Finishing Technique

Preparation

- Cut 7 x 1.2m (4ft) lengths of 5mm (³⁄₁₆in) natural cotton rope
- Cut 36 x 2m (6½ft) lengths of 5mm (³⁄₁₆in) natural cotton rope
- Cut 1 x 4m (13¼ft) length of 5mm (³⁄₁₆in) colour 1 cotton rope
- Cut 1 x 4m (13¼ft) length of 5mm (³⁄₁₆in) colour 2 cotton rope

Macramé Element

1. Secure the ends of one of the 1.2m (4ft) lengths of rope to the vertical rails of a clothes rack so that it lies horizontally; alternatively, secure to a project board or to a flat surface (see Mounting Techniques). This becomes your holding cord (see Essential Terminology).

2. Mount the thirty-six 2m (6½ft) lengths of rope onto the holding cord using horizontal double half hitches, leaving cord ends 10cm (4in) above the holding cord. Cords should be mounted to the centre of the holding cord, with the width of the mounted rope being approximately 30cm (12in).

3. Directly beneath the row of double half hitches, tie a row of nine half knots.

4. Alternate cords (see Essential Terminology) and tie a row of eight half knots.

5. Alternate cords and tie a row of nine half knots.

6. Continue an alternating half knot pattern for a further four rows.

7. Place a 1.2m (4ft) length of rope horizontally directly beneath the last row of knots. This is now the holding cord.

8. Tie horizontal double half hitches with all thirty-six cords along the holding cord.

9. Drop down 2.5cm (1in) and place another 1.2m (4ft) length of rope horizontally to become a holding cord.

10. Tie horizontal double half hitches with all thirty-six cords along the holding cord. This creates negative space 1 that will be used as the warp for your weave in step 22.

11. Drop down 2cm (¾in) and tie a row of six 6-cord square knots using one working cord on either side and four filler cords in the middle.

12. Alternate cords, drop down 2cm (¾in) and tie a row of five 6-cord square knots.

13. Alternate cords, drop down 2cm (¾in) and tie a row of six 6-cord square knots

14. Drop down 2cm (¾in) and place a 1.2m (4ft) length of rope horizontally. This is now the holding cord.

15. Tie horizontal double half hitches with all thirty-six cords along the holding cord and weave in holding cord ends.

16. Drop down 2.5cm (1in) and place a 1.2m (4ft) length of rope horizontally to become a holding cord.

17. Tie horizontal double half hitches with all thirty-six cords along the holding cord. This creates negative space 2 that will be used as the warp for your weave in step 24.

18. Place another 1.2m (4ft) length of rope horizontally to become a holding cord directly beneath the last row of double half hitches.

19. Tie horizontal double half hitches with all thirty-six cords along the holding cord.

20. Repeat steps 18 and 19.

21. Trim the working cord ends to 25cm (10in) and tie each off with an overhand knot.

Weaving Element

22. Using the 4m (13¼ft) length of 5mm (³⁄₁₆in) colour 1 rope as your weft thread, soumak weave through negative space 1 for two rows.

23. Bring the leftover cord ends around to the back of the weave and use a weaving finishing technique to secure.

24. Using the 4m (13¼ft) length of 5mm (³⁄₁₆in) colour 2 rope as your weft thread, tabby weave through negative space 2 for three rows.

25. Bring the leftover cord end around to the back of the weave. Secure the cord ends on the back of the weave using a weaving finishing technique.

26. Secure the ends of all holding cords through the back of the design with a weaving finishing technique.

27. Trim the 10cm (4in) cord ends at the top of the panel to 5cm (2in) and secure with a weaving finishing technique to the back of the design; alternatively, use a hot glue gun to secure the cord ends in place.

28. Whip stitch the finished panel onto the front of your cushion cover.

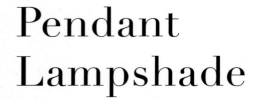

Pendant Lampshade

The macraweave technique is ideal for lampshades of all sizes, softly filtering light through the design, so who could resist making this large-scale pendant as an eye-catching focal point for any room? A central band of sisal soumak weave naturally complements the square knot macramé sections worked with hemp for results that are stunningly beautiful.

Materials

- 168m (560ft) of 5mm (³⁄₁₆in) hemp
- 125m (412½ft) of 3mm (⅛in) sisal
- 40cm (15¾in) drum lampshade powder-coated metal ring set with two rings, one with light holder fitting and one without*
- Three 40cm (15¾in) metal rings

Note: Choose the appropriate fitting type in accordance with your country's standard

Techniques

- Double Reverse Lark's Head Knot
- Square Knot
- Alternating Square Knot Pattern
- Double Half Hitch
- Numbering Cords
- Joining Weaving Cords
- Soumak Weave
- Weaving Finishing Technique

Preparation

- Cut 56 x 3m (10ft) lengths of 5mm (³⁄₁₆in) hemp
- Cut 25 x 5m (16½ft) lengths of 3mm (⅛in) sisal

Macramé Element

1. Secure the powder-coated ring with light holder fitting to a horizontal rail so the ring is sitting straight and vertical. This ring will now be used as the holding cord.

2. Attach the fifty-six 3m (10ft) lengths of hemp to the ring with double reverse lark's head knots.

3. Secure the hemp cords to the ring by tying a row of twenty-eight square knots directly beneath the ring.

4. Alternate cords (see Essential Terminology), drop down 1.5cm (⅝in) and tie another row of twenty-eight square knots.

5. Continue an alternating square knot pattern for another two rows dropping down 1.5cm (⅝in) between each row.

6. Take one of the 40cm (15¾in) metal rings and place all cords inside. This metal ring sitting horizontally is now to be used as the holding cord. Tie all cords onto the metal ring using double half hitches.

7. Drop down 9.5cm (3¾in) and place all cords inside a second 40cm (15¾in) metal ring. Tie all cords onto the metal ring using double half hitches, making sure each cord is dropped down 9.5cm (3¾in) before tying it to the ring to ensure the second ring is parallel to the one above it. This creates a negative space that will be used as the warp for your weave in steps 14–18.

8. Directly beneath the last row of double half hitches, tie a row of twenty-eight square knots.

9. Continue with an alternating square knot pattern for another three rows dropping down 1.5cm (⅝in) between each row.

10. Place all cords inside a third 40cm (15¾in) metal ring. This metal ring sitting horizontally is now to be used as the holding cord. Tie all cords onto the metal ring using double half hitches.

11. Place all cords inside the last of the 40cm (15¾in) metal rings (the powder-coated one that came with the drum lampshade metal ring set). This metal ring sitting horizontally is now to be used as the holding cord. Tie all cords onto the metal ring using double half hitches, directly beneath the last row of double half hitches.

12. Trim cords to 7cm (2¾in) and fray.

Weaving Element

13. Returning to the negative space, number the cords 1 to 112 and get ready to start weaving from the bottom to the top.

14. Join together five 5m (16½ft) lengths of sisal (to be used as your weft thread). Beginning at the left of cords 1 and 2, leave an end of 20cm (8in) on the inside of the ring and soumak weave using a two over two under pattern. Weave from left to right completing a full row.

15. Join together five 5m (16½ft) lengths of sisal. Beginning at the right of cords 57 and 58, leave an end of 20cm (8in) on the inside of the ring and soumak weave using a two over two under pattern. Weave from right to left completing a full row.

16. Join together five 5m (16½ft) lengths of sisal. Beginning at the left of cords 29 and 30, leave an end of 20cm (8in) on the inside of the ring and soumak weave using a two over two under pattern. Weave from left to right completing a full row.

17. Join together five 5m (16½ft) lengths of sisal. Beginning at the right of cords 85 and 86, leave an end of 20cm (8in) on the inside of the ring and soumak weave using a two over two under pattern. Weave from right to left, completing a full row.

18. Join together five 5m (16½ft) lengths of sisal twine. Beginning at the left of cords 15 and 16, leave an end of 20cm (8in) on the inside of the ring and soumak weave using a two over two under pattern. Weave from left to right completing a full row.

19. Use a weaving finishing technique to weave in cord ends through the back of the design on the inside of the lampshade.

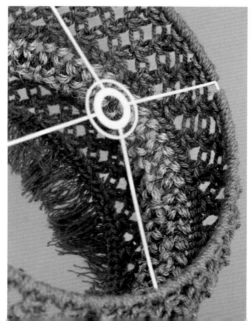

Plant Cradle

Emphasise the natural beauty of your foliage with this elegantly woven plant holder which can be hung from the ceiling by its delicately wrapped hanging ring. The straps of the cradle are made with a simple yet stunning design of alternating square knot pattern followed by tabby weave sections making this an ideal way to perfect your new weaving skills. Substitute your plant for a tray and this becomes a very handy hanging table!

Materials

- 77.5m (256½ft) of 5mm (³⁄₁₆in) natural cotton rope
- 24m (80ft) of 5mm (³⁄₁₆in) coloured cotton rope
- 40cm (15¾in) of 3mm (⅛in) natural cotton rope
- 17cm (7in) metal ring
- 13cm (5in) metal ring

Techniques

- Wrapping a Ring
- Reverse Lark's Head Knot
- Alternating Square Knot Pattern
- Overhand Knot
- Wrapped Knot
- Tabby Weave
- Weaving Finishing Technique

Preparation

- Cut 1 x 3m (10ft) length of 5mm (³⁄₁₆in) natural cotton rope
- Cut 16 x 4m (13¼ft) lengths of 5mm (³⁄₁₆in) natural cotton rope
- Cut 1 x 2.5m (8¼ft) length of 5mm (³⁄₁₆in) natural cotton rope
- Cut 1 x 8m (26¼ft) length of 5mm (³⁄₁₆in) natural cotton rope
- Cut 1 x 40cm (15¾in) length of 3mm (⅛in) natural cotton rope
- Cut 16 x 1.5m (5ft) lengths of 5mm (³⁄₁₆in) coloured cotton rope

Macramé Element

Note: The macramé for the plant cradle is completed from the bottom upwards. The cords are first mounted onto the larger ring, which is the base where the plant pot sits, and each of the four straps are then tied before looping the cords over the smaller ring and securing with a wrapped knot.

1. Wrap the 17cm (7in) metal ring with the 3m (10ft) length of 5mm (³⁄₁₆in) natural rope cutting the excess cord off as close as possible.

2. Mount the sixteen 4m (13¼ft) lengths of 5mm (³⁄₁₆in) natural rope onto the ring with reverse lark's head knots so that the cords are placed in four groups of eight cords at the 12 o'clock, 3 o'clock, 6 o'clock and 9 o'clock positions. Each group now becomes a sinnet (see Essential Terminology). You can either secure the ring to a rack, or work on a flat surface, repeating steps 3–7 for each sinnet.

3. Tie three rows of alternating square knot pattern directly beneath the ring.

4. Drop down 10cm (4in) and tie three rows of alternating square knot pattern. This will create a negative space that will be used as the warp for your weave in step 15.

5. Drop down 10cm (4in) and tie three rows of alternating square knot pattern to create another negative space.

6. Drop down 10cm (4in) and tie three rows of alternating square knot pattern to create another negative space.

7. Drop down 10cm (4in) and this time tie four rows of alternating square knot pattern to finish the sinnet with a one square knot row, creating another negative space.

8. Place one sinnet side by side with an adjacent sinnet. Number the cords 1 to 16 (see Numbering the Cords) and tie a square knot with cords 7 to 10 to join together the sinnets.

9. Repeat step 8 with the remaining two sinnets. You will now have only two sinnets. Trim the ends of both sinnets to 30cm (12in) in length.

10. Wrap the 13cm (5in) metal ring with the 2.5m (8¼ft) length of 5mm (³⁄₁₆in) natural rope.

11. Take the cord ends of one of the sinnets and fold them in half over the inside of the wrapped ring, then repeat to fold the ends of the second sinnet in the opposite direction on top.

12. Gather together all cords and wrap with the 40cm (15¾in) length of 3mm (⅛in) natural rope just beneath the metal ring, firmly tying with a double overhand knot to secure in place.

13. Using the 8m (26¼ft) length of natural rope, tie a wrapped knot 13cm (5in) long (or as long as necessary) to cover the cords, making sure that the double overhand knot is hidden.

14. Trim off any excess cords not covered by the wrapped knot, making sure that you do not not cut any necessary cords.

Weaving Element

15. You have created sixteen negative spaces on the plant hanger for the warp of the weave. Taking a 1.5m (5ft) length of the coloured rope as your weft thread, tabby weave through each of the negative spaces for approximately thirteen rows.

16. Use a weaving finishing technique to weave the ends in.

Rainbow Arch Wall Hanging

Materials

- 21.5m (71ft) of 8mm (⁵⁄₁₆in) natural cotton rope
- 25.2m (79½ft) of 5mm (³⁄₁₆in) natural cotton rope
- 13m (43ft) of 5mm (³⁄₁₆in) colour 1 (light pink) cotton rope
- 6.5m (21½ft) of 5mm (³⁄₁₆in) colour 2 (yellow) cotton rope
- 11.5m (38¼ft) of 5mm (³⁄₁₆in) colour 3 (light brown) cotton rope
- 7m (23¼ft) of 5mm (³⁄₁₆in) colour 4 (pink) cotton rope
- 16m (52½ft) tapestry wool
- Chenille needle

Techniques

- Reverse Lark's Head Knot
- Wrapped Knot
- Tabby Weave
- Overhand Knot
- Whip Stitch
- Fraying

As a homage to Mother Nature herself, our rainbow arch is made using a natural cotton rope in a selection of earthy tones, creating a focal point to brighten up even the barest of walls. Bringing a touch of vintage charm to your room, this multi-layered piece is designed to challenge your construction skills to help you make a more intricate design, and so it makes an ideal intermediate level project.

Preparation

SMALL ARCH

- Cut 2 x 2m (6½ft) lengths of 8mm (⁵⁄₁₆in) natural cotton rope
- Cut 2 x 90cm (3ft) lengths of 5mm (³⁄₁₆in) natural cotton rope
- Cut 1 x 3m (10ft) length of 5mm (³⁄₁₆in) natural cotton rope
- Cut 1 x 2.5m (8¼ft) length of 5mm (³⁄₁₆in) colour 1 cotton rope
- Cut 1 x 1m (3¼ft) length of 5mm (³⁄₁₆in) colour 2 cotton rope
- Cut 1 x 4.5m (15ft) length of 5mm (³⁄₁₆in) colour 3 cotton rope

SMALL-MEDIUM ARCH

- Cut 2 x 2.5m (8¼ft) lengths of 8mm (⁵⁄₁₆in) natural cotton rope
- Cut 2 x 90cm (3ft) lengths of 5mm (³⁄₁₆in) natural cotton rope
- Cut 1 x 4m (13¼ft) length of 5mm (³⁄₁₆in) natural cotton rope
- Cut 1 x 4.5m (15ft) length of 5mm (³⁄₁₆in) colour 3 cotton rope
- Cut 1 x 1m (3¼ft) length of 5mm (³⁄₁₆in) colour 4 cotton rope
- Cut 1 x 3m (10ft) length of 5mm (³⁄₁₆in) colour 1 cotton rope

MEDIUM ARCH

- Cut 2 x 3m (10ft) lengths of 8mm (⁵⁄₁₆in) natural cotton rope
- Cut 2 x 90cm (3ft) lengths of 5mm (³⁄₁₆in) natural cotton rope
- Cut 1 x 4.5m (15ft) length of 5mm (³⁄₁₆in) natural cotton rope
- Cut 1 x 4.5m (15ft) length of 5mm (³⁄₁₆in) colour 2 cotton rope
- Cut 1 x 3m (10ft) length of 5mm (³⁄₁₆in) colour 4 cotton rope
- Cut 1 x 2.5m (8¼ft) length of 5mm (³⁄₁₆in) colour 1 cotton rope

LARGE ARCH

- Cut 2 x 3.25m (10¾ft) lengths of 8mm (⁵⁄₁₆in) natural cotton rope
- Cut 2 x 90cm (3ft) lengths of 5mm (³⁄₁₆in) natural cotton rope
- Cut 1 x 4m (13¼ft) length of 5mm (³⁄₁₆in) natural cotton rope
- Cut 1 x 2.5m (8¼ft) length of 5mm (³⁄₁₆in) natural cotton rope
- Cut 1 x 2.5m (8¼ft) length of 5mm (³⁄₁₆in) colour 3 cotton rope
- Cut 1 x 1m (3¼ft) length of 5mm (³⁄₁₆in) colour 2 cotton rope
- Cut 1 x 3m (10ft) length of 5mm (³⁄₁₆in) colour 4 cotton rope
- Cut 1 x 5m (16½ft) length of 5mm (³⁄₁₆in) colour 1 cotton rope

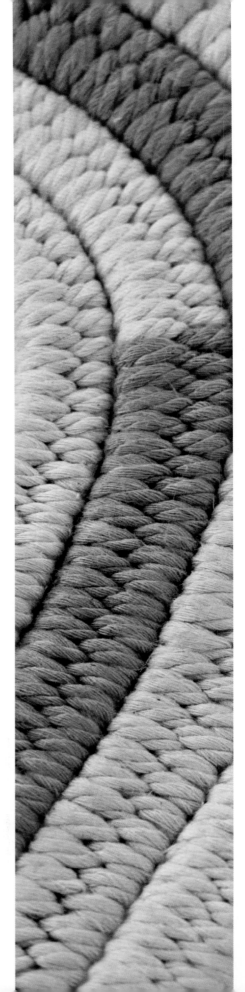

Macramé Element

Steps 1–4 are macramé for the small arch

1. Attach two 2m (6½ft) lengths of 8mm (⁵⁄₁₆in) rope to a horizontal bar with a diameter no thicker than 2cm (¾in) using reverse lark's head knots placed side by side.

2. Drop down 5cm (2in) and tie a 4cm (1½in) wrapped knot using a 90cm (3ft) length of 5mm (³⁄₁₆in) natural rope. Cut off cord ends so they are unseen. This will be the top wrapped knot.

3. Drop down 43cm (17in) and tie a 4cm (1½in) wrapped knot using a 90cm (3ft) length of 5mm (³⁄₁₆in) natural rope. Cut off cord ends so they are unseen. This will be the bottom wrapped knot.

4. Make sure all four cords hanging down are straight and not overlapping each other. The cords between the top and bottom wrapped knots create a negative space that will be used as the warp for your weave. Trim the ends below the bottom wrapped knot to 15cm (6in).

Steps 5–8 are macramé for the small-medium arch

5. Attach two 2.5m (8¼ft) lengths of 8mm (⁵⁄₁₆in) rope to a horizontal bar with a diameter no thicker than 2cm (¾in) using reverse lark's head knots placed side by side.

6. Drop down 5cm (2in) and tie a 4cm (1½in) wrapped knot using a 90cm (3ft) length of 5mm (³⁄₁₆in) natural rope. Cut off cord ends so unseen. This will be the top wrapped knot.

7. Drop down 52cm (20½in) and tie a 4cm (1½in) wrapped knot using a 90cm (3ft) length of 5mm (³⁄₁₆in) natural rope. Cut off cord ends so they are unseen. This will be the bottom wrapped knot.

8. Make sure all four cords hanging down are straight and not overlapping each other. The cords between the top and bottom wrapped knots create a negative space that will be used as the warp for your weave. Trim the ends below the bottom wrapped knot to 15cm (6in).

Steps 9–12 are macramé for the medium arch

9. Attach two 3m (10ft) lengths of 8mm (⁵⁄₁₆in) rope to a horizontal bar with a diameter no thicker than 2cm (¾in) using reverse lark's head knots placed side by side.

10. Drop down 5cm (2in) and tie a 4cm (1½in) wrapped knot using a 90cm (3ft) length of 5mm (³⁄₁₆in) natural rope. Cut off cord ends so they are unseen. This will be the top wrapped knot.

11. Drop down 60cm (23⅝in) and tie a 4cm (1½in) wrapped knot using a 90cm (3ft) length of 5mm (³⁄₁₆in) natural rope. Cut off cord ends so they are unseen. This will be the bottom wrapped knot.

12. Make sure all four cords hanging down are straight and not overlapping each other. The cords between the top and bottom wrapped knots create a negative space that will be used as the warp for your weave. Trim the ends below the bottom wrapped knot to 15cm (6in).

Steps 13–16 are macramé for the large arch

13. Attach two 3.25m (10¾ft) lengths of 8mm (⁵⁄₁₆in) rope to a horizontal bar with a diameter no thicker than 2cm (¾in) using reverse lark's head knots placed side by side.

14. Drop down 5cm (2in) and tie a 4cm (1½in) wrapped knot using a 90cm (3ft) length of 5mm (³⁄₁₆in) natural rope. Cut off cord ends so unseen. This will be the top wrapped knot.

15. Drop down 70cm (27¾in) and tie a 4cm (1½in) wrapped knot using a 90cm (3ft) length of 5mm (³⁄₁₆in) natural rope. Cut off cord ends so they are unseen. This will be the bottom wrapped knot.

16. Make sure all four cords hanging down are straight and not overlapping each other. The cords between the top and bottom wrapped knots create a negative space that will be used as the warp for your weave. Trim the ends below the bottom wrapped knot to 15cm (6in).

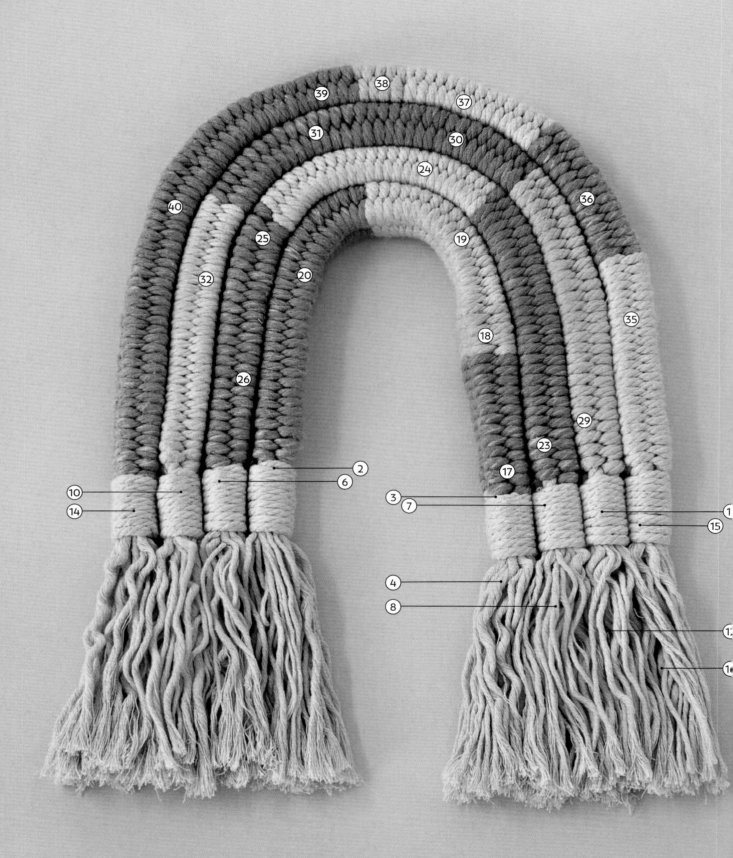

Weaving Element

Steps 17–22 are weaving for the small arch

17. Beginning at the bottom wrapped knot, place a 2.5m (8¼ft) length of 5mm (³⁄₁₆in) colour 1 rope (to be used as your weft thread) through the middle of the cords leaving a 10cm (4in) tail at the back. Weave weft through all four warp cords using a tabby weave and continue to weave upwards for approx. 10cm (4in) leaving a 10cm (4in) tail at the back.

18. Add a 1m (3¼ft) length of 5mm (³⁄₁₆in) colour 2 rope through the middle of the cords leaving a 10cm (4in) tail at the back. Weave weft through all four warp cords using a tabby weave and continue to weave upwards for approx. 3cm (1⅛in) leaving a 10cm (4in) tail at the back.

19. Add a 3m (10ft) length of 5mm (³⁄₁₆in) natural rope through the middle of the cords leaving a 10cm (4in) tail at the back. Weave weft through all four warp cords using a tabby weave and continue to weave upwards for approx. 12cm (4¾in) leaving a 10cm (4in) tail at the back.

20. Add a 4.5m (15ft) length of 5mm (³⁄₁₆in) colour 3 rope through the middle of the cords leaving a 10cm (4in) tail at the back. Weave weft through all four warp cords using a tabby weave and continue to weave upwards for approx. 18cm (7in) leaving a 10cm (4in) tail at the back.

21. The woven area should now be at the top wrapped knot, but if not simply add more rope and continue until it is. Tie off all tail ends with overhand knots and trim close.

22. Cut the loop at the back of the reverse lark's head knots to release the woven design from the bar.

Steps 23–28 are weaving for the small-medium arch

23. Beginning at the bottom wrapped knot, place a 4.5m (15ft) length of 5mm (³⁄₁₆in) colour 3 rope (to be used as your weft thread) through the middle of the cords leaving a 10cm (4in) tail at the back. Weave weft through all four warp cords using a tabby weave and continue to weave upwards for approx. 20cm (8in) leaving a 10cm (4in) tail at the back.

24. Add a 4m (13¼ft) length of 5mm (³⁄₁₆in) natural rope through the middle of the cords leaving a 10cm (4in) tail at the back. Weave weft through all four warp cords using a tabby weave and continue to weave upwards for approx. 17cm (6¾in) leaving a 10cm (4in) tail at the back.

25. Add a 1m (3¼ft) length of 5mm (³⁄₁₆in) colour 4 rope through the middle of the cords leaving a 10cm (4in) tail at the back. Weave weft through all four warp cords using a tabby weave and continue to weave upwards for approx. 3cm (1⅛in) leaving a 10cm (4in) tail at the back.

26. Add a 3m (10ft) length of 5mm (³⁄₁₆in) colour 1 rope through the middle of the cords leaving a 10cm (4in) tail at the back. Weave weft through all four warp cords using a tabby weave and continue to weave upwards for approx. 12cm (4¾in) leaving a 10cm (4in) tail at the back.

27. The woven area should now be at the top wrapped knot, but if not simply add more rope and continue until it is. Tie off all tail ends with overhand knots and trim close.

28. Cut the loop at the back of the reverse lark's head knots to release the woven design from the bar.

Steps 29–34 are weaving for the medium arch

29. Beginning at the bottom wrapped knot, place a 4.5m (15ft) length of 5mm (³⁄₁₆in) colour 2 rope (to be used as your weft thread) through the middle of the cords leaving a 10cm (4in) tail at the back. Weave weft through all four warp cords using a tabby weave and continue to weave upwards for approx. 20cm (8in) leaving a 10cm (4in) tail at the back.

30. Add a 3m (10ft) length of 5mm (³⁄₁₆in) colour 4 rope through the middle of the cords leaving a 10cm (4in) tail at the back. Weave weft through all four warp cords using a tabby weave and continue to weave upwards for approx. 12cm (4¾in) leaving a 10cm (4in) tail at the back.

31. Add a 2.5m (8¼ft) length of 5mm (³⁄₁₆in) colour 1 rope through the middle of the cords leaving a 10cm (4in) tail at the back. Weave weft through all four warp cords using a tabby weave and continue to weave upwards for approx. 10cm (4in) leaving a 10cm (4in) tail at the back.

32. Add a 4.5m (15ft) length of 5mm (³⁄₁₆in) natural rope through the middle of the cords leaving a 10cm (4in) tail at the back. Weave weft through all four warp cords using a tabby weave and continue to weave upwards for approx. 18cm (7in) leaving a 10cm (4in) tail at the back.

33. The woven area should now be at the top wrapped knot, but if not simply add more rope and continue until it is. Tie off all tail ends with overhand knots and trim close.

34. Cut the loop at the back of the reverse lark's head knots to release the woven design from the bar.

Steps 35–42 are weaving for the large arch

35. Beginning at the bottom wrapped knot, place a 4m (13¼ft) length of 5mm (³⁄₁₆in) natural rope (to be used as your weft thread) through the middle of the cords leaving a 10cm (4in) tail at the back. Weave weft through all four warp cords using a tabby weave and continue to weave upwards for approx. 15cm (6in) leaving a 10cm (4in) tail at the back.

36. Add a 2.5m (8¼ft) length of 5mm (³⁄₁₆in) colour 3 rope through the middle of the cords leaving a 10cm (4in) tail at the back. Weave weft through all four warp cords using a tabby weave and continue to weave upwards for approx. 10cm (4in) leaving a 10cm (4in) tail at the back.

37. Add a 2.5m (8¼ft) length of 5mm (³⁄₁₆in) natural rope through the middle of the cords leaving a 10cm (4in) tail at the back. Weave weft through all four warp cords using a tabby weave and continue to weave upwards for approx. 10cm (4in) leaving a 10cm (4in) tail at the back.

38. Add a 1m (3¼ft) length of 5mm (³⁄₁₆in) colour 2 rope through the middle of the cords leaving a 10cm (4in) tail at the back. Weave weft through all four warp cords using a tabby weave and continue to weave upwards for approx. 3cm (1⅛in) leaving a 10cm (4in) tail at the back.

39. Add a 3m (10ft) length of 5mm (³⁄₁₆in) colour 4 rope through the middle of the cords leaving a 10cm (4in) tail at the back. Weave weft through all four warp cords using a tabby weave and continue to weave upwards for approx. 12cm (4¾in) leaving a 10cm (4in) tail at the back.

40. Add a 5m (16½ft) length of 5mm (³⁄₁₆in) colour 1 rope through the middle of the cords leaving a 10cm (4in) tail at the back. Weave weft through all four warp cords using a tabby weave and continue to weave upwards for approx. 20cm (8in) leaving a 10cm (4in) tail at the back.

41. The woven area should now be at the top wrapped knot, but if not simply add more rope and continue until it is. Tie off all tail ends with overhand knots and trim close.

42. Cut the the loop at the back of the reverse lark's head knots to release the woven design from the bar.

Constructing the Rainbow Arch

43. Take the small arch woven strip and, with the back of the design facing up, fold it in half to conceal the overhand knots inside. Making sure that the colour bands are aligned, use a chenille needle threaded with tapestry wool to whip stitch the edges together.

44. Repeat step 43 for the woven designs of each of the remaining arches.

45. Place the arches to sit flush, one above the other with wrong sides facing up, making sure all top wrapped knots and all bottom wrapped knots are in alignment. For ease of manipulation, you can use needles or pins to secure the arches in place before stitching them together.

46. Starting with the small arch and the small-medium arch, whip stitch together, first running a line of glue in between the arches to further secure them in place. Now attach the medium arch to the small-medium arch in the same way, then the large arch to the medium arch to complete your rainbow.

47. Trim the ends of the 8mm (5⁄16in) warp cords if desired and fray.

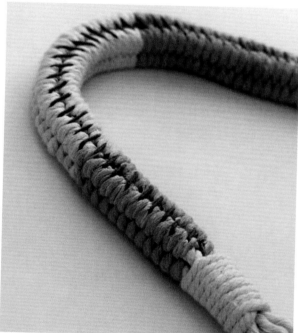

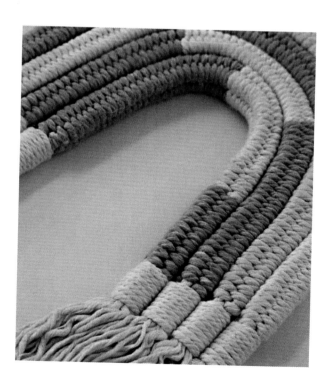

Zigzag Belt

Add a touch of style and sophistication to the simplest of outfits with this distinctively shaped belt. The natural beauty of hemp is combined with vibrantly coloured jute to make the stripes of the tabby weave panels, which are connected with delightfully textured triangular sections of diagonal double half hitches again in hard-wearing hemp. All in all, an essential accessory that is both pretty and practical.

Materials

- 20m (66ft) of 5mm (³⁄₁₆in) hemp
- 24m (78ft) of 3mm (⅛in) hemp
- 24m (80ft) each of 2mm (³⁄₃₂in) jute in two different colours of your choosing
- Wooden circular belt buckle with straight bar at least 5cm (2in) in length

Techniques

- Reverse Lark's Head Knot
- Numbering Cords
- Diagonal Double Half Hitch
- Overhand Knot
- Joining Weaving Cords
- Tabby Weave
- Adding Weaving Cords
- Weaving Finishing Technique

Preparation

- Cut 4 x 5m (16½ft) lengths of 5mm (³⁄₁₆in) hemp
- Cut 12 x 2m (6½ft) lengths of 3mm (⅛in) hemp
- Cut 16 x 1.5m (5ft) lengths of 2mm (³⁄₃₂in) jute in colour 1
- Cut 16 x 1.5m (5ft) lengths of 2mm (³⁄₃₂in) jute in colour 2

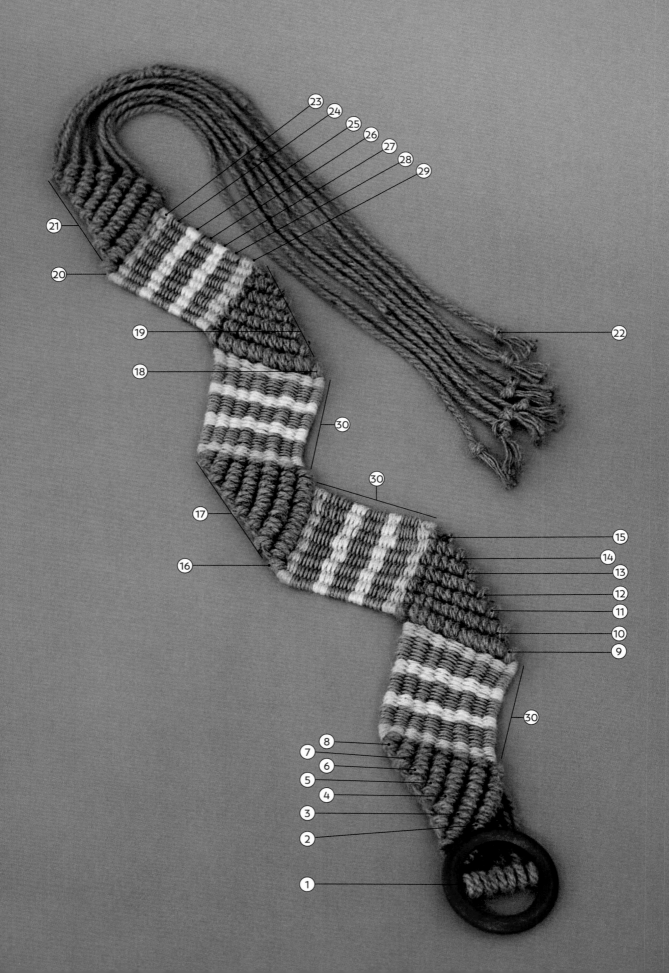

Macramé Element

1. Mount the four 5m (16½ft) lengths of 5mm (³⁄₁₆in) hemp onto the straight bar of the belt buckle using reverse lark's head knot.

2. Number the cords 1 to 8. Make cord 8 a holding cord (see Essential Terminology), bring it down right to left and tie diagonal double half hitches onto it with cords 1–7.

3. Renumber cords 1 to 8. Make cord 8 a holding cord, bring it down right to left directly beneath the previous row of double half hitches and tie diagonal double half hitches onto it with cords 2–7.

4. Renumber cords 1 to 8. Make cord 8 a holding cord, bring it down right to left directly beneath the previous row of double half hitches and tie diagonal double half hitches onto it with cords 3–7.

5. Renumber cords 1 to 8. Make cord 8 a holding cord, bring it down right to left directly beneath the previous row of double half hitches and tie diagonal double half hitches onto it with cords 4–7.

6. Renumber cords 1 to 8. Make cord 8 a holding cord, bring it down right to left directly beneath the previous row of double half hitches and tie diagonal double half hitches onto it with cords 5–7.

7. Renumber cords 1 to 8. Make cord 8 a holding cord, bring it down right to left directly beneath the previous row of double half hitches and tie diagonal double half hitches onto it with cords 6 and 7

8. Renumber cords 1 to 8. Make cord 8 a holding cord, bring it down right to left directly beneath the previous row of double half hitches and tie a diagonal double half hitch onto it with cord 7.

9. Renumber cords 1 to 8. Drop cord 1 down 10cm (4in). Make cord 1 a holding cord, bring it down left to right and tie diagonal double half hitches onto it with cords 2–8. This creates negative space 1 that will be used as the warp for your weave in step 30.

10. Renumber cords 1 to 8. Make cord 1 a holding cord, bring it down left to right directly beneath the previous row of double half hitches and tie diagonal double half hitches onto it with cords 2–7.

11. Renumber cords 1 to 8. Make cord 1 a holding cord, bring it down left to right directly beneath the previous row of double half hitches and tie diagonal double half hitches onto it with cords 2–6.

12. Renumber cords 1 to 8. Make cord 1 a holding cord, bring it down left to right directly beneath the previous row of double half hitches and tie diagonal double half hitches onto it with cords 2–5.

13. Renumber cords 1 to 8. Make cord 1 a holding cord, bring it down left to right directly beneath the previous row of double half hitches and tie diagonal double half hitches onto it with cords 2–4.

14. Renumber cords 1 to 8. Make cord 1 a holding cord, bring it down left to right directly beneath the previous row of double half hitches and tie diagonal double half hitches onto it with cords 2 and 3.

15. Renumber cords 1 to 8. Make cord 1 a holding cord, bring it down left to right directly beneath the previous row of double half hitches and tie a diagonal double half hitch onto it with cord 2.

16. Renumber cords 1 to 8. Drop cord 8 down 10cm (4in). Make cord 8 a holding cord, bring it down right to left and tie diagonal double half hitches onto it with cords 1–7. This creates negative space 2 that will be used as the warp for your weave in step 30.

17. Repeat steps 3–8.

18. Renumber cords 1 to 8. Drop cord 1 down 10cm (4in). Make cord 1 a holding cord, bring it down 10cm left to right and tie diagonal double half hitches onto it with cords 2–8. This creates negative space 3 that will be used as the warp for your weave in step 30.

19. Repeat steps 10–15.

20. Renumber cords 1 to 8. Drop cord 8 down 10cm (4in). Make cord 8 a holding cord, bring it down right to left and tie diagonal double half hitches onto it with cords 1–7. This creates negative space 4 that will be used as the warp for your weave in steps 23–29.

21. Repeat steps 3–8.

22. Trim ends to desired length and finish each with an overhand knot

Weaving Element

Note: If you wish, you can tie the ends of the belt tightly across the bottom of your clothes rack so the warp (hemp) cords of the negative spaces are taut for weaving. Attach the belt buckle to a clothes rack.

23. Begin weaving in negative space 4. Join together two 1.5m (5ft) lengths of 2mm (³⁄₃₂in) jute in colour 1 (to be used as your weft thread) and tabby weave for six rows or 1cm (³⁄₈in).

24. Add a 2m (6½ft) length of 3mm (⅛in) hemp and tabby weave for 12 rows or 2cm (¾in).

25. Join together two 1.5m (5ft) lengths of 2mm (³⁄₃₂in) jute in colour 2 and tabby weave for six rows or 1cm (³⁄₈in).

26. Add a 2m (6½ft) length of 3mm (⅛in) hemp and tabby weave for 12 rows or 2cm (¾in).

27. Join together two 1.5m (5ft) lengths of 2mm (³⁄₃₂in) jute in colour 2 and tabby weave for six rows or 1cm (³⁄₈in).

28. Add a 2m (6½ft) length of 3mm (⅛in) hemp and tabby weave for 12 rows or 2cm (¾in).

29. Join together two 1.5m (5ft) lengths of 2mm (³⁄₃₂in) jute in colour 1 and tabby weave for six rows or 1cm (³⁄₈in), or until the negative space is completely woven.

30. For negative space 3, negative space 2 and negative space 1, repeat the weaving as described in steps 23–29.

31. Use a weaving finishing technique to weave in all ends through the back of the design.

Feather Fray Earrings

Accessorise to the finest with a pair of attention-grabbing earrings. Incorporating earthy tones, a long fray and gold feature beads, these delightful adornments will add a touch of glamour whatever the occasion, from coffee shop gatherings to celebration galas. Worked on a basic jump ring with cotton yarns, the knotting and weaving techniques may be familiar but require some dexterity to create the intricate design.

Materials

Quantities given are to make a pair of earrings

- 6.8m (22½ft) of 1mm (⅟₃₂in) cotton yarn in colour 1
- 19m (63½ft) of 1mm (⅟₃₂in) cotton yarn in colour 2
- Two 1cm (⅜in) jump rings
- Thirty-two crimp beads with a 1mm (⅟₃₂in) bead hole minimum
- Tapestry needle with blunt tip
- Two earring fish hooks
- Flat nose jewellery pliers

Techniques

- Reverse Lark's Head Knot
- Numbering Cords
- Diagonal Double Half Hitch
- Double Half Hitch
- Horizontal Double Half Hitch
- Square Knot
- Tabby Weave
- Weaving Finishing Technique
- Rya Knots

Preparation

Quantities given are to make a pair of earrings

- Cut 16 x 35cm (13¾in) lengths of 1mm (⅟₃₂in) cotton yarn in colour 1
- Cut 4 x 30cm (12in) lengths of 1mm (⅟₃₂in) cotton yarn in colour 1
- Cut 2 x 1.5m (5ft) lengths of 1mm (⅟₃₂in) cotton yarn in colour 2
- Cut 80 x 20cm (8in) lengths of 1mm (⅟₃₂in) cotton yarn in colour 2

Macramé Element

1. Secure the jump ring to a project board using a T-pin.

2. Mount eight 35cm (13¾in) lengths of 1mm (⅟₃₂in) colour 1 yarn onto the jump ring using reverse lark's head knots.

3. Number the cords 1 to 16.

4. Make cord 1 a holding cord, bring it down from left to right directly beneath the reverse lark's head knots and tie a row of diagonal double half hitches onto it with cords 2–8.

5. Repeat step 4 using cord 16 as your holding cord and cords 15–9 as your working cords.

6. Cross over holding cords 1 and 16 and tie a double half hitch using cord 16 as the holding cord and cord 1 as the working cord.

7. Thread a crimp bead onto each cord and push beads up against the last row of double half hitches.

8. Place a 30cm (12in) length of 1mm (⅟₃₂in) colour 1 yarn horizontally in an arc shape directly beneath the row of beads, leaving 7cm (2¾in) cord ends. This is now the holding cord.

9. Tie horizontal double half hitches with all cords along the holding cord maintaining an even 5mm (³⁄₁₆in) deep arc shape.

10. Drop down 5mm (³⁄₁₆in) and place another 30cm (12in) length of 1mm (⅟₃₂in) colour 1 yarn horizontally in the same arc shape as the previous row, leaving 7cm (2¾in) cord ends. This is now the holding cord.

11. Pull the 7cm (2¾in) cord ends down from the previous holding cord and tie a row of horizontal double half hitches with all cords along the current holding cord. This creates negative space 1 that will be used as the warp for your weave in step 13.

12. Drop down 2mm (³⁄₃₂in) and tie a row of five square knots. This creates negative space 2 that will be used as the warp for your weave in step 15.

Weaving Element

13. Thread the tapestry needle with a 1.5m (5ft) length of 1mm (⅟₃₂in) colour 2 yarn (to be used as your weft thread) and tabby weave through negative space 1 in a two over two under pattern for 5mm (³⁄₁₆in) or until completely woven.

14. Use a weaving finishing technique to weave in cord ends through the back of the design.

15. Divide forty 20cm (8in) lengths of 1mm (⅟₃₂in) colour 2 yarn into ten groups of four threads (to be used as your weft thread). Working in negative space 2 from left to right, place each group of four threads together evenly and tie a row of ten rya knots, each over two warp threads. Adjust the square knots if required to secure the rya knots firmly in place.

Completing the Earrings

16. Make a second earring following steps 1–15, then trim the thread ends into your desired shape.

17. Using a pair of flat nose jewellery pliers, attach an earring hook to each of the jump rings and your earrings are ready to wear.

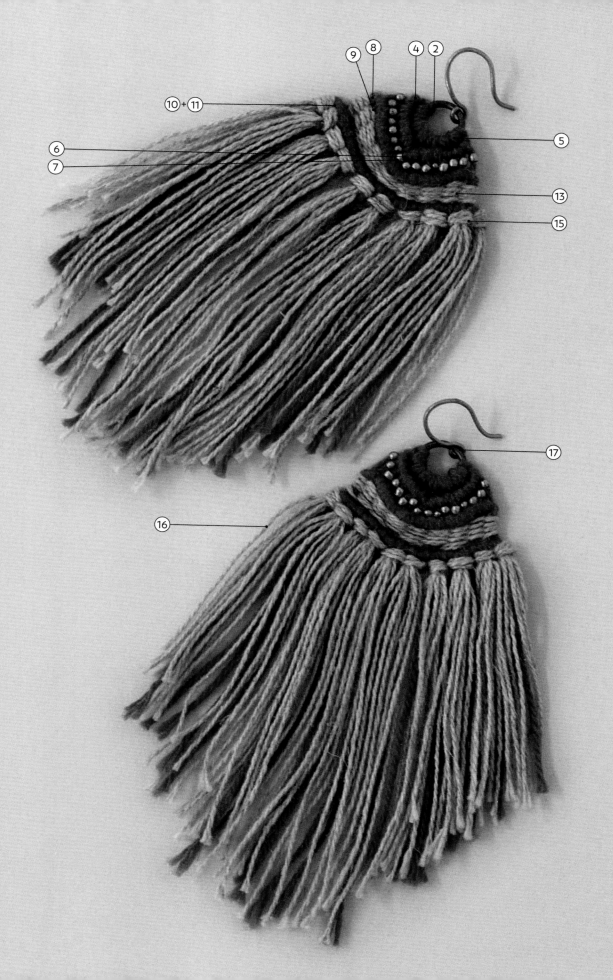

Collar
Necklace

This flattering necklace has been designed to fall on the collarbone and is guaranteed to steal the show. Created using multi-layered yarn in earthy tones woven through natural cotton, it is finished with the new edition square knot button and a long fray. A must-have accessory that will have you turning heads whatever the event.

Materials

- 17.75m (70¾ft) of 2mm (³⁄₃₂in) twisted cotton string
- 9.6m (32ft) of 1mm (¹⁄₃₂in) cotton yarn in colour 1
- 4.8m (16ft) of 1mm (¹⁄₃₂in) cotton yarn in colour 2
- Tapestry needle with blunt tip

Techniques

- Overhand Knot
- Plaiting
- Reverse Lark's Head Knot
- Double Half Hitch
- Square Knot Button
- Soumak Weave
- Tabby Weave
- Weaving Finishing Technique
- Fraying

Preparation

- Cut 3 x 1m (3¼ft) lengths of 2mm (³⁄₃₂in) twisted cotton string
- Cut 36 x 40cm (15¾in) lengths of 2mm (³⁄₃₂in) twisted cotton string
- Cut 1 x 35cm (13¾in) length of 2mm (³⁄₃₂in) twisted cotton string
- Cut 4 x 2.4m (8ft) lengths of 1mm (¹⁄₃₂in) colour 1 cotton yarn
- Cut 2 x 2.4m (8ft) lengths of 1mm (¹⁄₃₂in) colour 2 cotton yarn

Macramé Element

1. Leaving a 5cm (2in) cord end, join the three 1m (3¼ft) lengths of 2mm (³⁄₃₂in) twisted cotton string with an overhand knot.

2. Secure the overhand knot vertically to a flat surface using adhesive tape, then plait the secured lengths of twisted cotton string together for 80cm (31½in). Finish the plait by tying an overhand knot and trim ends to 5cm (2in).

3. Placing the plait horizontally and working 35cm (13¾in) from each end, secure it onto a project board using T-pins, or to a flat surface using adhesive tape (see Mounting Techniques). This becomes your holding cord (see Essential Terminology).

4. Mount the thirty-six 40cm (15¾in) lengths of 2mm (³⁄₃₂in) twisted cotton string onto the plait using reverse lark's head knots.

5. Drop down 1.5cm (⅝in). Take the 35cm (13¾in) length of 2mm (³⁄₃₂in) twisted cotton string and secure it horizontally onto the project board, using T-pins or adhesive tape. This now becomes the holding cord.

6. Leaving cord ends of 7cm (2¾in), tie double half hitches with all cords along the holding cord, then weave in the holding cord ends using the weaving finishing technique. This creates a negative space that will be used as the warp for your weave in steps 8–12.

7. Tie a row of eighteen square knot buttons directly beneath the row of double half hitches, spacing them 7mm (⁹⁄₃₂in) apart to leave space to tuck in the cords.

Weaving Element

8. Take two 2.4m (8ft) lengths of 1mm (¹⁄₃₂in) colour 1 cotton yarn (to be used as your weft thread) and thread both pieces evenly through the eye of the tapestry needle, pulling them all the way through until the ends meet evenly. You now have four even lengths of 1.2m (4ft) yarn.

9. Using the threaded needle, soumak weave through the negative space for one row. Use a weaving finishing technique to weave in cord ends through the back of the design.

10. Take two 2.4m (8ft) lengths of 1mm (¹⁄₃₂in) colour 2 cotton yarn (to be used as your weft thread) and thread both pieces evenly through the eye of the tapestry needle, pulling them all the way through until the ends meet evenly. You now have four even lengths of 1.2m (4ft) yarn.

11. Directly above your soumak weave row, use the threaded needle to tabby weave through the negative space in a two over two under pattern for one row. Use a weaving finishing technique to weave in cord ends through the back of the design.

12. Repeat steps 8 and 9 directly above the tabby weave row.

13. To finish the necklace, trim the cords beneath the square knot button row to the desired length and fray, using the photograph as a guide.

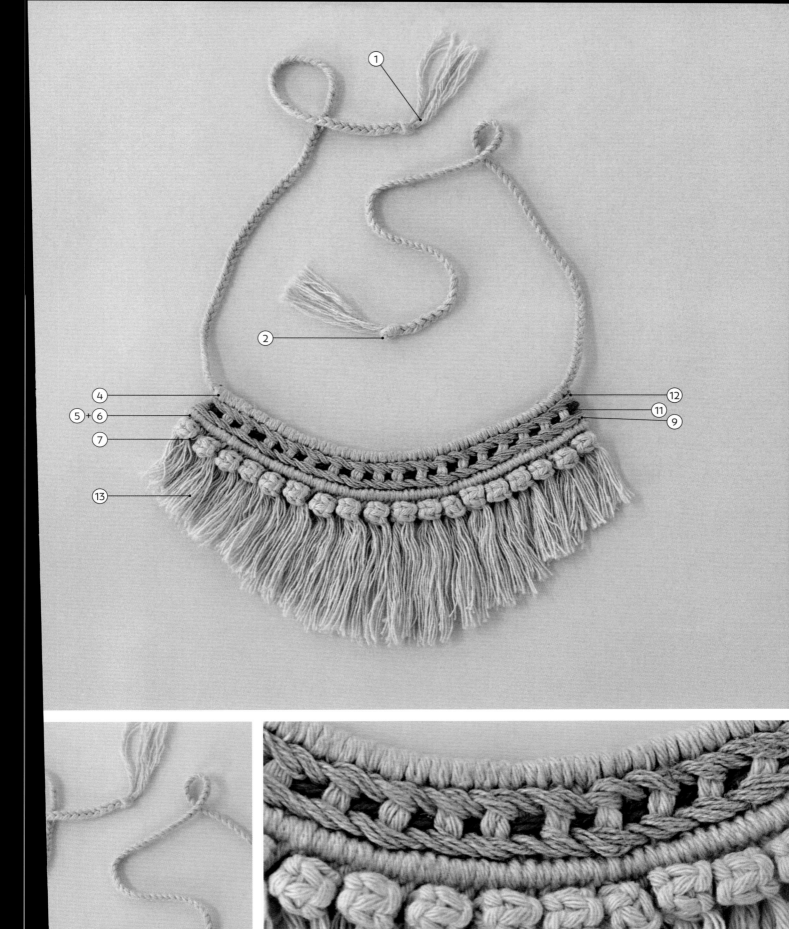

Lots of Pots Plant Holder

This beautiful, large-scale plant holder is created using the same method as a large wall hanging but the cords are brought inwards to form a cradle for a plant pot. It will provide the perfect hanging home for five of your favourite plants, and is sure to be a welcome addition to your living space.

Materials

- 192m (636ft) of 6mm (¼in) natural cotton rope
- 5m (16¼ft) of 5mm (³⁄₁₆in) natural cotton rope
- 2.5m (8½ft) of 3mm (⅛in) natural cotton rope
- 25.5m (84½ft) of 3cm (1⅛in) wide lace*
- 1.15m (3¾ft) length of thick driftwood

Note: Alternatively, use 3cm (1⅛in) wide fabric strips

Techniques

- Reverse Lark's Head Knot
- Square Knot
- Numbering Cords
- Diagonal Double Half Hitch
- Double Half Hitch
- Wrapped Knot
- Overhand Knot
- Tabby Weave
- Weaving Finishing Technique

Preparation

- Cut 24 x 5m (16½ft) lengths of 6mm (¼in) cotton rope
- Cut 16 x 4.5m (15ft) lengths of 6mm (¼in) cotton rope
- Cut 5 x 1m (3¼ft) lengths of 5mm (³⁄₁₆in) cotton rope
- Cut 5 x 50cm (20in) lengths of 3mm (⅛in) cotton rope
- Cut 2 x 1m (3¼ft) lengths of 3cm (1⅛in) lace
- Cut 12 x 1.5m (5ft) lengths of 3cm (1⅛in) lace
- Cut 1 x 5.5m (18ft) length of 3cm (1⅛in) lace

Macramé Element

1. Starting 25cm (10in) from the left-hand end of your length of driftwood and working from left to right, use reverse lark's head knots to mount the 6mm (¼in) lengths of cotton rope onto the hanger in the following order: eight 5m (16½ft) lengths, eight 4.5m (15ft) lengths, eight 5m (16½ft) lengths, eight 4.5m (15ft) lengths, eight 5m (16½ft) lengths.

2. Directly beneath the driftwood, tie a row of twenty square knots.

3. Drop down 4cm (1½in) from the lowest point of your driftwood and number the cords 1 to 80.

4. Make cord 9 a holding cord, bring it down right to left and tie diagonal double half hitches onto it with cords 1–7.

5. Make cord 8 a holding cord, bring it down left to right and tie diagonal double half hitches onto it with cords 10–16.

6. Make cord 25 a holding cord, bring it down right to left and tie diagonal double half hitches onto it with cords 17–23.

7. Make cord 24 a holding cord, bring it down left to right and tie diagonal double half hitches onto it with cords 26–32.

8. Make cord 41 a holding cord, bring it down right to left and tie diagonal double half hitches onto it with cords 33–39.

9. Make cord 40 a holding cord, bring it down left to right and tie diagonal double half hitches onto it with cords 42–48.

10. Make cord 57 a holding cord, bring it down right to left and tie diagonal double half hitches onto it with cords 49–55.

11. Make cord 56 a holding cord, bring it down left to right and tie diagonal double half hitches onto it with cords 58–64.

12. Make cord 73 a holding cord, bring it down right to left and tie diagonal double half hitches onto it with cords 65–71.

13. Make cord 72 a holding cord, bring it down left to right and tie diagonal double half hitches onto it with cords 74–80. You will now have created negative space 1 that will be used as the warp for your weave in steps 76–82.

14. Renumber the cords 1 to 80.

15. Tie a double half hitch with cord 16 onto cord 17.

16. Tie a double half hitch with cord 32 onto cord 33.

17. Tie a double half hitch with cord 48 onto cord 49.

18. Tie a double half hitch with cord 64 onto cord 65.

19. Drop down approx. 4cm (1½in) from the top point of the diamond (where the diagonal double half hitches meet). Using cords 4–13, tie a 10-cord square knot using cords 4–6 and 11–13 as working cords and cords 7–10 as filler cords. When positioning the square knot keep in mind that you want this to sit in the centre of your diamond shape.

20. Drop down approx. 4cm (1½in) from the top point of the diamond. Using cords 20–29, tie a 10-cord square knot using cords 20–22 and 27–29 as working cords and cords 23–26 as filler cords.

21. Drop down approx. 4cm (1½in) from the top point of the diamond. Using cords 36–45, tie a 10-cord square knot using cords 36–38 and 43–45 as working cords and cords 39–42 as filler cords.

22. Drop down approx. 4cm (1½in) from the top point of the diamond. Using cords 52–61, tie a 10-cord square knot using cords 52–54 and 59–61 as working cords and cords 55–58 as filler cords.

23. Drop down approx. 4cm (1½in) from the top point of the diamond. Using cords 68–77, tie a 10-cord square knot using cords 68–70 and 75–77 as working cords and cords 71–74 as filler cords.

24. Make cord 1 a holding cord, bring it down left to right and tie diagonal double half hitches onto it with cords 2–8.

25. Make cord 16 a holding cord, bring it down right to left and tie diagonal double half hitches onto it with cords 9–15.

26. Make cord 17 a holding cord, bring it down left to right and tie diagonal double half hitches onto it with cords 18–24.

27. Make cord 32 a holding cord, bring it down right to left and tie diagonal double half hitches onto it with cords 25–31.

28. Make cord 33 a holding cord, bring it down left to right and tie diagonal double half hitches onto it with cords 34–40.

29. Make cord 48 a holding cord, bring it down right to left and tie diagonal double half hitches onto it with cords 41–47.

30. Make cord 49 a holding cord, bring it down left to right and tie diagonal double half hitches onto it with cords 50–56.

31. Make cord 64 a holding cord, bring it down right to left and tie diagonal double half hitches onto it with cords 57–63.

32. Make cord 65 a holding cord, bring it down left to right and tie diagonal double half hitches onto it with cords 66–72.

33. Make cord 80 a holding cord, bring it down right to left and tie diagonal double half hitches onto it with cords 73–79.

34. Renumber the cords 1 to 80.

35. Tie a double half hitch with cord 8 onto cord 9.

36. Tie a double half hitch with cord 24 onto cord 25.

37. Tie a double half hitch with cord 40 onto cord 41.

38. Tie a double half hitch with cord 56 onto cord 57.

39. Tie a double half hitch with cord 72 onto cord 73.

40. Drop down approx. 4cm (1½in) from the top point of the diamond. Using cords 12–21, tie a 10-cord square knot using cords 12–14 and 19–21 as working cords and cords 15–18 as filler cords.

41. Drop down approx. 4cm (1½in) from the top point of the diamond. Using cords 28–37, tie a 10-cord square knot using cords 28–30 and 35–37 as working cords and cords 31–34 as filler cords.

42. Drop down approx. 4cm (1½in) from the top point of the diamond. Using cords 44–53, tie a 10-cord square knot using cords 44–46, 51–53 as working cords and cords 47–50 as filler cords.

43. Drop down approx. 4cm (1½in) from the top point of the diamond. Using cords 60–69 tie a 10-cord square knot using cords 60–62 and 67–69 as working cords and cords 63–66 as filler cords.

44. Make cord 8 a holding cord, bring it down right to left and tie diagonal double half hitches onto it with cords 1–7. You will now have created negative space 2 that will be used as the warp for your weave in step 84.

45. Make cord 9 a holding cord, bring it down left to right and tie diagonal double half hitches onto it with cords 10–16.

46. Make cord 24 a holding cord, bring it down right to left and tie diagonal double half hitches onto it with cords 17–23.

47. Make cord 25 a holding cord, bring it down left to right and tie diagonal double half hitches onto it with cords 26–32.

48. Make cord 40 a holding cord, bring it down right to left and tie diagonal double half hitches onto it with cords 33–39.

49. Make cord 41 a holding cord, bring it down left to right and tie diagonal double half hitches onto it with cords 42–48.

50. Make cord 56 a holding cord, bring it down right to left and tie diagonal double half hitches onto it with cords 49–55.

51. Make cord 57 a holding cord, bring it down left to right and tie diagonal double half hitches onto it with cords 58–64.

52. Make cord 72 a holding cord, bring it down right to left and tie diagonal double half hitches onto it with cords 65–71.

53. Make cord 73 a holding cord, bring it down left to right and tie diagonal double half hitches onto it with cords 74–80. You will now have created negative space 3 that will be used as the warp for your weave in step 84.

54. Repeat steps 15–39 to create the next row of diamonds.

55. Repeat steps 44 and 45. This will create negative spaces 4 and 5.

56. Repeat steps 48 and 49. This will create negative spaces 6 and 7.

57. Repeat steps 52 and 53. This will create negative spaces 8 and 9.

58. Drop down approx. 4cm (1½in) from the top point of the diamond. Using cords 4–13, tie a 10-cord square knot using cords 4–6 and 11–13 as working cords and cords 7–10 as filler cords.

59. Drop down approx. 4cm (1½in) from the top point of the diamond. Using cords 36–45, tie a 10-cord square knot using cords 36–38 and 43–45 as working cords and cords 39–42 as filler cords.

60. Drop down approx. 4cm (1½in) from the top point of the diamond. Using cords 68–77, tie a 10-cord square knot using cords 68–70 and 75–77 as working cords and cords 71–74 as filler cords.

61. Make cord 1 a holding cord, bring it down left to right and tie diagonal double half hitches onto it with cords 2–8.

62. Make cord 16 a holding cord, bring it down right to left and tie diagonal double half hitches onto it with cords 9–15.

63. Tie a double half hitch with cord 8 onto cord 9.

64. Make cord 33 a holding cord, bring it down left to right and tie diagonal double half hitches onto it with cords 34–40.

65. Make cord 48 a holding cord, bring it down right to left and tie diagonal double half hitches onto it with cords 41–47.

66. Tie a double half hitch with cord 40 onto cord 41.

67. Make cord 65 a holding cord, bring it down left to right and tie diagonal double half hitches onto it with cords 66–72.

68. Make cord 80 a holding cord, bring it down right to left and tie diagonal double half hitches onto it with cords 73–79.

69. Tie a double half hitch with cord 72 onto cord 73.

70. Separate cords into five groups of sixteen cords: group 1 – cords 1–16; group 2 – cords 17–32; group 3 – cords 33–48; group 4 – cords 49–64; group 5 – cords 65–80. Complete steps 71–75 on each of the five groups to create the five plant pot hanging enclosures.

71. Drop down 11cm (4¼in) from the bottom of the centre point of the diamond and tie a horizontal row of four square knots.

72. Drop down 5cm (2in), alternate cords (see Essential Terminology) and tie three square knots.

73. For the fourth and final square knot in the row, bring together cords 1–2 and 15–16 (that is the first two and the last two cords in the group) into the centre and to the front, and tie a square knot in line with the square knots in the row of diamonds above it.

74. Drop down 7cm (2¾in). Bring all the cords in the group together and firmly secure with a triple overhand knot using a 50cm (20in) length of 3mm (⅛in) cotton rope.

75. Using a 1m (3¼ft) length of 5mm (³⁄₁₆in) cotton rope, cover the 3mm (⅛in) rope with a 4cm (1½in) wrapped knot. Trim cords to the desired length using the photograph as your guide.

Weaving Element for Negative Space 1

76. Beginning on the left-hand side of the design, use a 1m (3¼ft) length of lace as your weft thread to tabby weave from the lowest point of the negative space upwards only until the peak of the diamond shape.

77. Move across to the next lowest point and use a 1.5m (5ft) length of lace as your weft thread to tabby weave from the lowest point of the negative space upwards only until the peak of the diamond shape.

78. Move across to the next lowest point and use a 1.5m (5ft) length of lace as your weft thread to tabby weave from the lowest point of the negative space upwards only until the peaks of the diamond shapes.

79. Move across to the next lowest point and use a 1.5m (5ft) length of lace as your weft thread to tabby weave from the lowest point of the negative space upwards only until the peaks of the diamond shapes.

80. Move across to the next lowest point and use a 1.5m (5ft) length of lace as your weft thread to tabby weave from the lowest point of the negative space upwards only until the peaks of the diamond shapes.

81. Move across to the next lowest point and use a 1m (3¼ft) length of lace as your weft thread to tabby weave from the lowest point of the negative space upwards only until the peak of the diamond shape.

82. Use the 5.5m (18ft) length of lace as your weft thread to tabby weave the remaining area of negative space 1 until it is completely woven.

83. Use a weaving finishing technique to weave the ends of the lace in through the back of the design.

Weaving Element for Negative Spaces 2–9

84. Use a 1.5m (5ft) length of lace as your weft thread to tabby weave through each of the remaining eight negative spaces.

85. Use a weaving finishing technique to weave the ends of the lace in through the back of design.

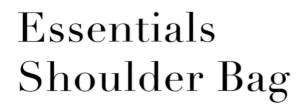

Essentials
Shoulder Bag

Perfect for your next beach getaway or girls' day out, this gorgeous '70s style handbag is made from cotton rope with an eye-catching woven diamond design flap. It's certain to draw attention and, best of all, you can put it in the wash after all the use it will be getting!

Materials

- 104m (344ft) of 6mm (¼in) natural cotton rope
- 5m (16½ft) of 4mm (⁵⁄₃₂in) natural cotton rope
- 3m (10ft) of 3mm (⅛in) natural cotton rope
- 30cm (12in) of 2mm (³⁄₃₂in) natural cotton rope
- Metal snap fastener (optional)

Techniques

- Double Reverse Lark's Head Knot
- Square Knot
- Alternating Square Knot Pattern
- Numbering Cords
- Decreasing Square Knot Pattern
- Diagonal Double Half Hitch
- Tabby Weave
- Joining Weaving Cords
- Weaving Finishing Technique
- Lacing Up
- Double Overhand Knot
- Plaiting
- Wrapped Knot

Preparation

- Cut 22 x 4m (13¼ft) lengths of 6mm (¼in) cotton rope
- Cut 2 x 6.5m (21¼ft) lengths of 6mm (¼in) cotton rope
- Cut 1 x 3m (10ft) length of 6mm (¼in) cotton rope
- Cut 1 x 5m (16½ft) length of 4mm (⁵⁄₃₂in) cotton rope
- Cut 3 x 1m (3¼ft) lengths of 3mm (⅛in) cotton rope
- Cut 1 x 30cm (12in) length of 2mm (³⁄₃₂in) cotton rope

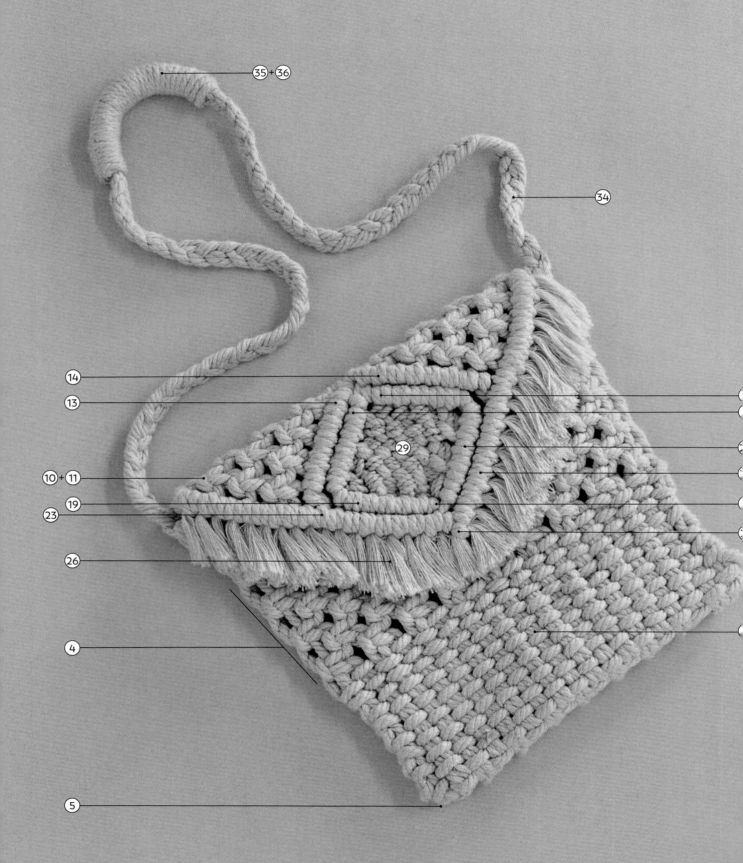

Macramé Element

1. Take two 4m (13¼ft) lengths of 6mm (¼in) rope and attach them to the vertical poles of a clothes rack so that they lie horizontally with the centre point of the rope in the centre of the rack. Now take the 3m (10ft) length of 6mm (¼in) rope and also attach it to the vertical poles of the rack, again making sure the centre point of the rope is in the centre. These three cords together will be used as a single holding cord.

2. Mount eighteen 4m (13¼ft) lengths of 6mm (¼in) rope onto the holding cord using double reverse lark's head knots, attaching them to the centre of the holding cord.

3. Directly beneath, tie a row of nine square knots.

4. Working directly beneath each row and alternating cords each time, tie eight rows of alternating square knot pattern.

5. Drop down 12cm (4¾in) and tie a row of nine square knots. This creates negative space 1 that will be used as the warp for your weave in step 27.

6. Drop down 12cm (4¾in) and tie a row of nine square knots. This creates negative space 2 that will be used as the warp for your weave in step 28.

7. Working directly beneath each row and alternating cords each time, tie eight rows of alternating square knot pattern.

8. Take two 4m (13¼ft) lengths of 6mm (¼in) rope and attach them to the vertical poles of the clothes rack, making sure that the centre point of the rope is in the centre of the rack and sitting just below the last row of square knots. These two pieces of rope together will now become a holding cord. Tie all thirty-six cords onto the holding cord using double half hitches. You will now begin working on the flap of the bag.

9. Number the cords 1 to 36. Tie a row of eight square knots, leaving out cords 17–20.

10. Renumber the cords 1 to 36. Separate the cords into two groups of sixteen cords: group 1 – cords 1–16; group 2 cords – 21–36.

11. On each of the two groups, work a decreasing square knot pattern beginning with four square knots and finishing with one in the last row.

12. Number the cords 1 to 36.

13. Make cord 19 a holding cord, bring it down right to left and tie diagonal double half hitches onto it with cords 10–17.

14. Make cord 18 a holding cord, bring it down left to right and tie diagonal double half hitches onto it with cords 20–27

15. Renumber cords 1 to 36.

16. Make cord 19 a holding cord, bring it down right to left and tie diagonal double half hitches onto it with cords 12-17

17. Make cord 18 a holding cord, bring it down left to right and tie diagonal double half hitches onto it with cords 20–25

18. Renumber cords 1 to 36.

19. Make cord 12 a holding cord, bring it down left to right and tie diagonal double half hitches onto it with cords 13–18.

20. Make cord 25 a holding cord, bring it down right to left and tie diagonal double half hitches onto it with cords 19–24.

21. Cross over holding cords 12 and 25.

22. Renumber cords 1–36.

23. Make cord 1 a holding cord, bring it down left to right and tie diagonal double half hitches onto it with cords 2–18.

24. Make cord 36 a holding cord, bring it down right to left and tie diagonal double half hitches onto it with cords 19–35.

25. Tie a double half hitch with cord 1 onto cord 36. This will complete your diamond shape and creates negative space 3 that will be used as the warp for your weave in step 29.

Weaving Element

27. Using a 6.5m (21¼ft) length of 6mm (¼in) rope as your weft thread, tabby weave through negative space 1.

28. Using a 6.5m (21¼ft) length of 6mm (¼in) rope as your weft thread, tabby weave through negative space 2.

29. Join together three 1m (3¼ft) lengths of 3mm (⅛in) rope to use as your weft thread, and tabby weave through negative space 3.

30. Use a weaving finishing technique to weave in cord ends through the back of the design.

Constructing the Bag

31. Untie the lengths of rope that are attached to the vertical poles of your clothes rack (tied on in steps 1 and 8). These will be used to lace up the bag sides and to make the shoulder strap.

32. Place the macramé on your work surface, wrong side up with the flap at the top as shown in the photo. Fold the bottom edge A (the row of double reverse lark's head knots) upwards by approx. 25cm (10in) so it meets the back side of the row of double half hitches B (tied in step 8). This will create the bag pocket.

33. Use the 3m (10ft) holding cord from step 1 to lace up the sides of the bag pocket referring to Techniques: Lacing Up for the macramé sections; when you get to the woven part of the pocket, simply continue to do the same, weaving from one side of the pocket to the other, passing through the middle of the first and second warps. Finish with the holding cord on the inside of the bag and secure with a double overhand knot.

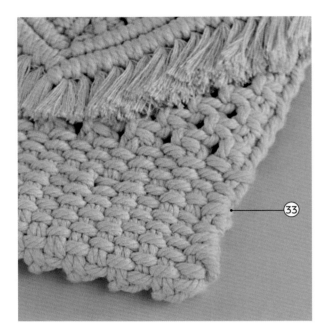

34. You now have four cords remaining on either side of the bag and these will be the starting points for the shoulder strap. Working first from one side, separate the four cords into one cord, one cord and two cords, and work a tight plait 60cm (2ft) long. Plait the four cords on the other side in the same way.

35. To start to make the handle, overlap the ends of the plaited straps by 12cm (4¾in), making sure that one sits flat on top of the other. Gather together all cords and use the 30cm (12in) length of 2mm (³⁄₃₂in) rope to tie a double overhand knot at the centre of the overlapping straps.

36. Using the 5m (16½ft) length of 4mm (⁵⁄₃₂in) rope, tie a wrapped knot 15cm (6in) long to cover the double overhand knot, which should be at the centre of the wrapped knot. Trim off all excess cords.

37. Attach the metal snap fastener to complete the bag, securing one half to the inside of the bag flap and the other half to the front of the bag pocket.

fold up from A to meet B

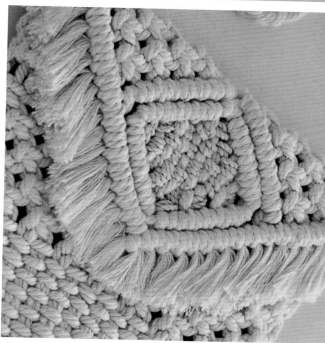

Give It a Whirl Coasters

Whether displaying a set of your finest wine glasses or providing a resting place for your favourite coffee cup, these simple yet classic coasters are the perfect addition to your table. Cords radiate from a Chinese crown knot to be mounted onto a ring and then woven to create a stylish circle design.

Materials

- 8.1m (26¾ft) of 3mm (⅛in) natural cotton rope
- 4m (13¼ft) of 4mm (⁵⁄₃₂in) natural cotton rope
- 13cm (5in) metal ring

Techniques

- Wrapping a Ring
- Chinese Crown Knot
- Double Half Hitch
- Soumak Weave
- Weaving Finishing Technique

Preparation

- Cut 1 x 2.5m (8¼ft) length of 3mm (⅛in) cotton rope
- Cut 8 x 70cm (27⅝in) lengths of 3mm (⅛in) cotton rope
- Cut 1 x 4m (13¼ft) length of 4mm (⁵⁄₃₂in) cotton rope

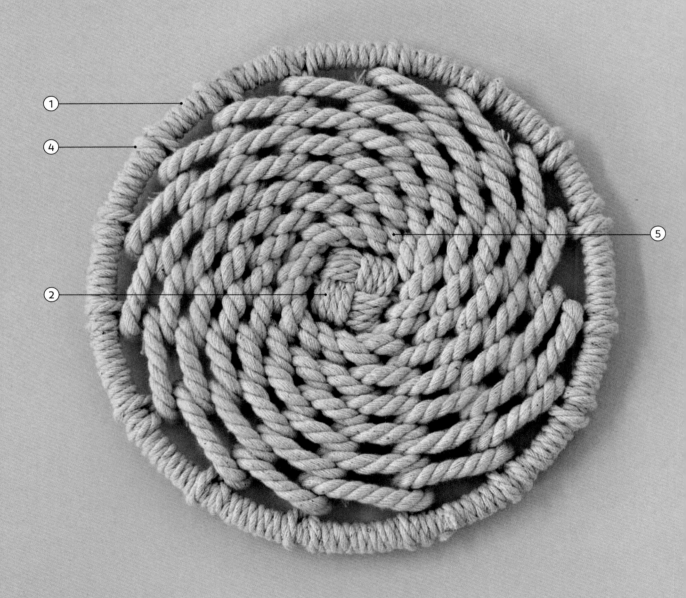

Macramé Element

1. Wrap the 13cm (5in) ring with the 2.5m (8¼ft) length of 3mm (⅛in) rope and set aside.

2. Divide the eight 70cm (27⅝in) lengths of 3mm (⅛in) rope into two groups of four cords, and lay each group down on a flat surface so they cross over at the centre. Tie a Chinese crown knot to secure the two groups of cords together. You now have four groups of four cords radiating out from what will become the centre of the coaster.

3. Separate the sixteen single cords so they are radiating outwards from the centre of the design. Take the 13cm (5in) wrapped ring and place it on top of the cords, ensuring the Chinese crown knot is in the centre of the ring and the cords are evenly spaced around the ring.

4. Tie all cords onto the ring with double half hitches, ensuring the spaces between each cord are even all the way around. This creates a negative space that will be used as the warp for your weave in step 5. Trim all cord ends to 4cm (1½in).

Weaving Element

5. Starting directly beneath the Chinese crown knot in the centre of the design and using the 4m (13¼ft) length of 4mm (⁵⁄₃₂in) rope as your weft thread, begin a soumak weave in a two over two under pattern. Work around in a clockwise direction and continue until you have completely woven the negative space.

6. Use a weaving finishing technique to weave in all ends into the back of the design.

Star Attraction Placemat

Add a touch of bohemian chic to your special event with this exquisite macraweave placemat. Make one as a centrepiece or, if you're feeling very creative, a whole set. The tight circular jute design offers great protection for your table.

Materials

- 70m (232¼ft) of 3mm (⅛in) jute
- 76.8m (256ft) of 5mm (³⁄₁₆in) jute
- 25cm (10in) metal ring
- Hot glue gun

Techniques

- Wrapping a Ring
- Chinese Crown Knot
- Square Knot
- Adding Cords with Square Knot
- Double Half Hitch
- Double Reverse Lark's Head Knot
- Decreasing Square Knot Pattern
- Diagonal Double Half Hitch
- Joining Weaving Cords
- Soumak Weave
- Adding Weaving Cords

Preparation

- Cut 1 x 6m (19¾ft) length of 3mm (⅛in) jute
- Cut 16 x 1.5m (5ft) lengths of 3mm (⅛in) jute
- Cut 10 x 4m (13¼ft) lengths of 3mm (⅛in) jute
- Cut 64 x 1.2m (4ft) lengths of 5mm (³⁄₁₆in) jute

Macramé Element

1. Wrap the 25cm (10in) ring with the 6m (19¾ft) length of 3mm (⅛in) jute, securing the cord ends with a hot glue gun.

2. Take eight 1.5m (5ft) lengths of 3mm (⅛in) jute and divide into two groups of four cords. Lay each group down on a flat surface so they cross over at the centre. Tie a Chinese crown knot to secure the two groups of cords together.

3. You now have four groups of four cords radiating out from what will become the centre of the placemat. Tie a square knot with each group of four cords, working a total of four square knots in all.

4. Take one working cord from one square knot together with one cord from its adjacent square knot, add one 1.5m (5ft) length of 3mm (⅛in) jute to it and tie a square knot (see Adding Cords with Square Knot: To Working Cords).

5. Repeat step 4 three times working around the centre, adding cords to the working cords of the other square knots. This will give you a total of eight square knots radiating out from the centre.

6. Using four 1.5m (5ft) lengths of 3mm (⅛in) jute, add cords by square knot to the filler cords of the square knots tied in step 3 (see Adding Cords with Square Knot: To Filler Cords).

7. Alternate cords (see Essential Terminology) and tie a row of eight square knots around the centre.

8. Separate the thirty-two single cords so they are radiating outwards from the centre of the design. Place the 25cm (10in) wrapped ring on top of the cords, ensuring the design is in the centre of the ring and the cords are evenly spaced around the ring.

9. Tie all cords onto the ring with double half hitches, ensuring the spaces between each cord are even all the way around. This creates a negative space that will be used as the warp for your weave in steps 19 and 20. Trim the thirty-two 3mm (⅛in) lengths of jute to 5cm (2in) (these cords will no longer be worked into the design and will be finished off in step 21).

10. Mount thirty-two 1.2m (4ft) lengths of 5mm (³⁄₁₆in) jute to the ring in between the trimmed 3mm (⅛in) cords, using double reverse lark's head knots.

11. Using the remaining 1.2m (4ft) lengths of 5mm (14in) jute, add thirty-two cords by square knot to the filler cords of the cords mounted in step 10.

12. Alternate cords and tie a row of thirty-two square knots directly beneath the last row.

13. Separate the cords into eight groups of sixteen cords: group 1 – cords 1–16; group 2 – cords 17–32; group 3 – cords 33–48; group 4 – cords 49–64; group 5 – cords 65–80; group 6 – cords 81–96; group 7 – cords 97–112, group 8 – 113–128. Complete steps 14–18 for each of the eight groups to create the points of the star.

14. Work a decreasing square knot pattern directly beneath the last row that you tied, beginning with four square knots and finishing with one square knot in the last row.

15. Number the cords 1 to 16. Make cord 1 a holding cord, bring it down left to right along the edge of the pattern and tie diagonal double half hitches onto the holding cord with cords 2–8.

16. Make cord 16 a holding cord bring it down right to left along the edge of the pattern and tie diagonal double half hitches onto the holding cord with cords 9–15

17. Tie a double half hitch with cord 1 onto cord 16 to secure them together.

18. Trim the cord ends to 4cm (1½in) and use a hot glue gun to secure them on the back of the design.

Weaving Element

19. Take five of the 4m (13¼ft) lengths of 3mm (⅛in) jute and join together (see Essential Terminology), to be used as your weft thread. Starting directly beneath one of the square knots in the centre of the design, begin to soumak weave working in a clockwise direction using a two over two under pattern. Continue to weave until you have a cord end of approx. 10cm (4in) remaining.

20. Join together the remaining five 4m (13¼ft) lengths of 3mm (⅛in) jute, adding the cords where you finished off in step 19, and continue to soumak weave as before to fill the ring.

21. Use a weaving finishing technique to weave in all ends into the back of the design.

Handy Clutch Purse

This purse is a casual yet stunning daily essential, which can go from a relaxed day-at-the-beach look to chic bohemian style with ease. With its multi-stranded pocket and woven flap, it is a very on-trend fashion accessory that is the perfect size for your phone, keys and wallet.

Materials

- 160.5m (534¼ft) of 3mm (⅛in) jute
- 20m (65ft) of 1mm (¹⁄₃₂in) cotton yarn in a colour of your choosing
- Hot glue gun
- Metal snap fastener (optional)

Techniques

- Reverse Lark's Head Knot
- Half Knot
- Alternating Half Knot Pattern
- Double Half Hitch
- Joining Weaving Cords
- Tabby Weave
- Soumak Weave
- Weaving Finishing Technique
- Lacing Up
- Double Overhand Knot

Preparation

- Cut 1 x 2.5m (8¼ft) length of 3mm (⅛in) jute
- Cut 1 x 2m (6½ft) length of 3mm (⅛in) jute
- Cut 2 x 6m (19¾ft) lengths of 3mm (⅛in) jute
- Cut 48 x 3m (10ft) lengths of 3mm (⅛in) jute
- Cut 10 x 2m (6½ft) lengths of 1mm (¹⁄₃₂in) cotton yarn in your chosen colour

Macramé Element

1. Secure the 2.5m (8¼ft) length of 3mm (⅛in) jute horizontally to a project board with T-pins making sure it is straight and firm and leaving a 30cm (12in) tail at each side. This becomes your holding cord (see Essential Terminology).

2. Take two of the 3m (10ft) lengths of 3mm (⅛in) jute, place together, fold in half and mount onto your holding cord using a reverse lark's head knot. Repeat for the remaining forty-six 3m (10ft) lengths of 3mm (⅛in) jute.

3. Directly beneath your row of twenty-four reverse lark's head knots, tie a row of six 16-cord half knots using four working cords on either side and eight filler cords in the middle.

4. Alternate cords (see Essential Terminology) and tie a row of five 16-cord half knots using four working cords on either side and eight filler cords in the middle.

5. Continue a loose alternating half knot pattern with minimal spacing in between the rows for another twenty-one rows, ending with a row of six half knots. The total length of the macramé should be 26cm (10¼in). If necessary, work more rows to the required length, but remember that it is important to end on a row of six half knots.

6. Drop down 6cm (2⅜in) and separate the cords into twenty-four groups of four cords. Take the 2m (6½ft) length of 3mm (⅛in) jute and tie each group of four cords along the length of it using double half hitches. This creates a negative space that will be used as the warp for your weave of the purse flap in steps 8–10.

7. Fold the ends of each group of four cords to the back of the flap, trim and glue down using a hot glue gun.

Weaving Element

8. Starting at the bottom of the flap and working your way to the top, begin to weave through the negative space. First join together five 2m (6½ft) lengths of 1mm (⅟32in) cotton yarn in your chosen colour (to be used as your weft thread) and tabby weave for one row in a two group over two group under pattern.

9. Join together the two 6m (19¾ft) lengths of 3mm (⅛in) jute and continue to soumak weave through the negative space in a two group over two group under pattern for approx. 3.5cm (1⅜in).

10. Join together the remaining five 2m (6½ft) lengths of 1mm (⅟32in) cotton yarn and continue with a tabby weave for one row, or until the negative space is fully woven, in a two group over two group under pattern.

11. Use a weaving finishing technique to weave in the cord ends into the back of the flap.

Constructing the Purse

12. Lay the piece wrong side facing up on your work surface with the flap at top. Fold the bottom edge up by 10cm (4in) to make the pocket of the purse.

13. Use the 30cm (12in) tails of the holding cord from step 1 to lace up the sides of the purse pocket, finishing with the cord on the inside of the purse, and secure with a double overhand knot.

14. Attach the metal snap fastener to complete the bag, securing one half to the inside of the bag flap and the other half to the front of the bag pocket.

Woven Wheel Mirror

Charm meets functionality in this beautiful macraweave mirror frame. Cords are mounted onto two rings in a circular pattern, then knotted and woven in eye-catching colours to create a statement piece suitable for any room.

Materials

- 160m (521ft) of 3mm (⅛in) natural hemp
- 40m (132½ft) of 2mm (³⁄₃₂in) natural hemp
- 58m (194½ft) of 2mm (³⁄₃₂in) hemp in colour 1
- 34m (115ft) of 2mm (³⁄₃₂in) hemp in colour 2
- Three cane, rattan or plastic rings: one 20cm (8in), one 36cm (14¼in), one 46cm (18⅛in)
- Hot glue gun
- Circular mirror at least 20cm (8in) in diameter

Techniques

- Reverse Lark's Head Knot
- Square Knot
- Double and Triple Half Hitch
- Joining Weaving Cords
- Tabby Weave
- Weaving Finishing Technique

Preparation

- Cut 48 x 2m (6½ft) lengths of 3mm (⅛in) natural hemp
- Cut 48 x 1m (3¼ft) lengths of 3mm (⅛in) natural hemp
- Cut 4 x 4m (13¼ft) lengths of 3mm (⅛in) natural hemp
- Cut 10 x 4m (13¼ft) lengths of 2mm (³⁄₃₂in) natural hemp
- Cut 20 x 1.7m (5¾ft) lengths of 2mm (³⁄₃₂in) colour 1 hemp
- Cut 6 x 4m (13¼ft) lengths of 2mm (³⁄₃₂in) colour 1 hemp
- Cut 20 x 1.7m (5¾ft) lengths of 2mm (³⁄₃₂in) colour 2 hemp

Macramé Element

1. Mount thirty-two 2m (6½ft) lengths of 3mm (⅛in) natural hemp onto the 20cm (8in) ring using reverse lark's head knots, placing the cords so there are four cords in eight groups equally spaced around the ring. Number each of the spaces in between the cord groups 1 to 8.

2. For each of the eight groups containing four cords, tie a sinnet (see Essential Terminology) of five 8-cord square knots, using two working cords on either side and four filler cords in the middle.

3. Place the 36cm (14¼in) ring on top of the cords, ensuring it is evenly spaced from the first ring all the way around and that each of the sinnets just reaches the ring. Tie each of the cords from the sinnets onto the ring using double half hitches.

4. Working in space 1, mount lengths of 3mm (⅛in) natural hemp to the 20cm (8in) ring using reverse lark's head knots in the following order: 2 x 1m (3¼ft), 4 x 2m (6½ft), 2 x 1m (3¼ft) (note where you attach the 2m (6½ft) lengths as you will need to locate them later).

5. Repeat step 4 in spaces 3, 5 and 7.

6. In space 2, mount eight 1m (3¼ft) lengths of 3mm (⅛in) natural hemp to the 20cm (8in) ring using reverse lark's head knots.

7. Repeat step 6 in spaces 4, 6 and 8.

8. Tie all new cords added in steps 4–7 onto the 36cm (14¼in) ring with double half hitches. This creates the eight negative spaces between the inner ring and the middle ring that will be used as the warp for your weave in steps 13–17.

9. Locate the four groups of the 2m (6½ft) cords attached in steps 4 and 5 and with each, tie a sinnet of three 8-cord square knots using two working cords on either side and four filler cords in the middle.

10. Place the 46cm (18⅛in) ring on top of the cords, ensuring it is evenly spaced from the second ring and that each of the four sinnets just reaches the ring. Tie each of the cords from the sinnets onto the ring using triple half hitches.

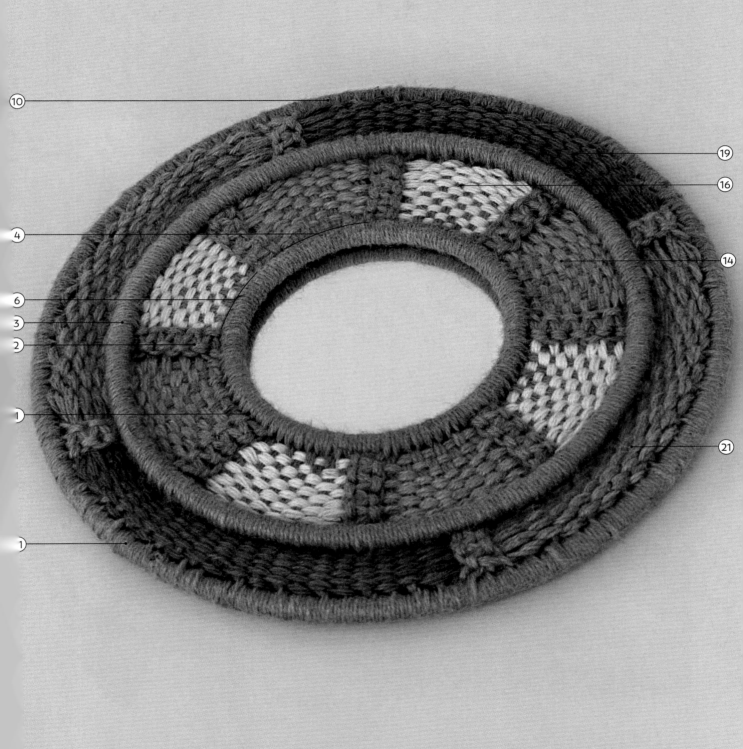

11. Now tie the remaining cords onto the 46cm (18⅛in) ring, again using triple half hitches. This creates the four negative spaces between the middle ring and the outer ring that will be used as the warp for your weave in steps 18–22.

12. Trim all cord ends to 10cm (4in) and glue to the back of the design with a hot glue gun.

Weaving Element

13. Begin by weaving the eight negative spaces between the inner ring and the middle ring. Number these negative spaces 1 to 8.

14. Join together five 1.7m (5¾ft) lengths of 2mm (³⁄₃₂in) colour 1 hemp (to be used as your weft thread). Tabby weave in negative space 1 for one row. Before continuing the second tabby weave row, weave the cords underneath the back of the square knot in line with the row (see detail photo). Continue to tabby weave until negative space 1 is completely woven, weaving through the back of the square knots with each completed row.

15. Repeat step 14 for negative spaces 3, 5 and 7.

16. Join together five 1.7m (5¾ft) lengths of 2mm (³⁄₃₂in) colour 2 hemp (to be used as your weft thread). Tabby weave in negative space 2 for one row. Before continuing the second tabby weave row, weave the cords underneath the back of the square knot in line with the row (see detail photo). Continue to tabby weave until negative space 2 is completely woven, weaving through the back of the square knots with each completed row.

17. Repeat step 16 for negative spaces 4, 6 and 8.

18. Now weave the four negative spaces between the middle ring and the outer ring. Number these negative spaces 1 to 4.

19. Join together five 4m (13¼ft) lengths of 2mm (³⁄₃₂in) natural hemp (to be used as your weft thread). Tabby weave in negative space 1 for one row. Before continuing the second tabby weave row, weave the cords underneath the back of the square knot in line with the row (see detail photo). Continue to tabby weave until negative space 1 is completely woven, weaving through the back of the square knots with each completed row.

20. Repeat step 19 for negative space 3.

21. Join together two 4m (13¼ft) lengths of 3mm (⅛in) hemp with three 4m (13¼ft) lengths of 2mm (³⁄₃₂in) colour 1 hemp (to be used as your weft thread). Tabby weave in negative space 2 for one row. Before continuing the second tabby weave row, weave the cords underneath the back of the square knot in line with the row (see detail photo). Continue to tabby weave until negative space 2 is completely woven, weaving through the back of the square knots with each completed row.

22. Repeat step 21 for negative space 4.

23. Use a weaving finishing technique to conceal the ends on the back of the design. Use a hot glue gun to affix the mirror to the design, ensuring it is centred to the ring.

Dress It Up
Flower Vase

Transform your cut-flower holders into works of art with this adaptable decoration. The macramé pattern is worked on your chosen container so it moulds perfectly to the shape of the piece, creating a bespoke item. A woven band in black cotton and jute brings earthy textures to this simple vessel reinvention.

Materials

- 31.1m (103½ft) of 5mm (³⁄₁₆in) natural cotton rope
- 7.8m (25½ft) of 2mm (³⁄₃₂in) jute
- 18m (60ft) of 3mm (⅛in) jute
- 2m (6½ft) of 3mm (⅛in) black cotton rope
- Vase of your choosing*

*Note: Our vase was 15cm (6in) high with a diameter of 13cm (5in) at the base and 10cm (4in) at the neck.

Techniques

- Overhand Knot
- Reverse Lark's Head Knot
- Square Knot
- Alternating Square Knot Pattern
- Double Half Hitch
- Wrapped Knot
- Fraying
- Joining Weaving Cords
- Soumak Weave
- Tabby Weave
- Weaving Finishing Technique

Preparation

- Cut 1 x 1.5m (5ft) length of 5mm (³⁄₁₆in) natural cotton rope
- Cut 23 x 1.2m (4ft) lengths of 5mm (³⁄₁₆in) natural cotton rope*
- Cut 2 x 1m (3¼ft) lengths of 5mm (³⁄₁₆in) natural cotton rope
- Cut 12 x 65cm (25½in) lengths of 2mm (³⁄₃₂in) jute
- Cut 6 x 3m (10ft) lengths of 3mm (⅛in) jute
- Cut 1 x 2m (6½ft) of 3mm (⅛in) black cotton rope

*Note: You can add or subtract cords accordingly but use an odd number.

Macramé Element

1. Take the 1.5m (5ft) length of 5mm (³⁄₁₆in) natural cotton rope and tie it loosely around the neck of your chosen bottle or vase with a temporary overhand knot, making sure the cord ends are even. This becomes your holding cord (see Essential Terminology).

2. Mount the twenty-three 1.2m (4ft) lengths of 5mm (³⁄₁₆in) natural cotton rope to the holding cord using reverse lark's head knots.

3. Take the two ends of the holding cord together with one cord from the left-hand side and one cord from the right-hand side and tie these four cords into a tight square knot.

4. Undo the temporary overhand knot you made in step 1. Continue to tie a further eleven knots to give you a row of twelve square knots in all.

5. Alternate cords (see Essential Terminology) and tie a row of twelve square knots.

6. Continue an alternating square knot pattern for another two rows.

7. Place a 1m (3¼ft) length of 5mm (³⁄₁₆in) natural cotton rope horizontally around the vase and directly beneath the last row of square knots. This now becomes the holding cord. Tie double half hitches with all cords onto the holding cord.

8. Tie a double half hitch knot with one end of the holding cord onto the other. Trim ends short to approx. 1cm (³⁄₈in) and tuck them up underneath the row of square knots above.

9. Drop down 3cm (1⅛in) and place the remaining 1m (3¼ft) length of 5mm (³⁄₁₆in) natural cotton rope horizontally around the vase. This now becomes the holding cord. Tie double half hitches with all cords onto the holding cord.

10. Tie a double half hitch knot with one end of the holding cord onto the other. This creates a negative space that will be used as the warp for your weave in steps 15–17. Trim ends short to approx. 1cm (³⁄₈in) and tuck them up into the negative space.

11. Separate the cords into twelve groups of four cords each.

12. Take a 65cm (25½in) length of 2mm (³⁄₃₂in) jute and tie a 1cm (³⁄₈in) wrapped knot around the first group of four cords.

13. Repeat step 12 for the remaining eleven groups of cords.

14. Trim the cords to the desired length and fray.

Weaving Element

15. Join together three 3m (10ft) lengths of 3mm (⅛in) jute (to be used as your weft thread) and soumak weave through the negative space for one row, working from left to right.

16. Using the 2m (6½ft) length of 3mm (⅛in) black cotton rope as your weft thread, tabby weave through the negative space for three rows. Once a complete row is woven, you will need to weave either over two warp threads or under two so that the second row is sitting in the opposite way to the first row.

17. Join together three 3m (10ft) lengths of 3mm (⅛in) jute (to be used as your weft thread) and soumak weave through the negative space for one row, working from right to left.

18. Use a weaving finishing technique to weave in cord ends through the back of the design.

Nursery Dream Catcher

This beautiful dream catcher is such a sweet accessory to adorn the walls of a child's room. The macramé pattern is made from the centre of the design spiralling outwards, starting from a tiny ring in the middle, and adding cords as you work your way to the outer ring. The tabby weave section can be adapted as you choose, to personalise the piece. After all, there is no right or wrong when it comes to creativity.

Materials

- 53.9m (178ft) of 5mm (³⁄₁₆in) natural cotton rope
- 30m (97¾ft) of 5mm (³⁄₁₆in) cotton rope in a colour of your choosing
- 12m (40ft) of 3mm (⅛in) sisal
- 1.5cm (⅝in) ring
- 35cm (13¾in) metal ring

Techniques

- Reverse Lark's Head Knot
- Half Knot
- Square Knot
- Weaving Finishing Technique
- Fraying
- Tabby Weave

Preparation

- Cut 1 x 5.5m (18ft) length of 5mm (³⁄₁₆in) natural cotton rope
- Cut 4 x 1.5m (5ft) lengths of 5mm (³⁄₁₆in) natural cotton rope
- Cut 12 x 1.2m (4ft) lengths of 5mm (³⁄₁₆in) natural cotton rope
- Cut 16 x 1m (3¼ft) lengths of 5mm (³⁄₁₆in) natural cotton rope*
- Cut 4 x 3m (10ft) lengths of 5mm (³⁄₁₆in) natural cotton rope
- Cut 1 x 5.5m (18ft) length of 5mm (³⁄₁₆in) cotton rope in your chosen colour
- Cut 1 x 2.5m (8¼ft) length of 5mm (³⁄₁₆in) cotton rope in your chosen colour
- Cut 22 x 1m (3¼ft) lengths of 5mm (³⁄₁₆in) cotton rope in your chosen colour*
- Cut 4 x 3m (10ft) lengths of 3mm (⅛in) sisal

*Note: Quantities include an extra four lengths for filling if necessary.

Macramé Element

1. Wrap the 35cm (13¾in) metal ring with the 5.5m (18ft) length of 5mm (³⁄₁₆in) natural cotton rope and set aside.

2. Take the four 1.5m (5ft) lengths of 5mm (³⁄₁₆in) natural cotton rope and mount each onto the 1.5cm (⅝in) ring using reverse lark's head knots.

3. Secure the middle of the ring to a project board using T-pins. This will now become your holding cord.

4. Separate the cords on the ring into four groups of two cords. Each group will now become your filler cords.

5. Take one of the 1.2m (4ft) lengths of 5mm (³⁄₁₆in) natural cotton rope and fold it in half. Place the folded rope behind one group of two filler cords so that there is one strand on either side of your filler cords, and these become your working cords. Make sure the ends of your working cords are even.

6. Push the working cords directly beneath the reverse lark's head knot and tie a half knot over the two filler cords, keeping the ring flat and the cords radiating outwards.

7. Repeat steps 5 and 6 for the remaining three groups of filler cords. You should now have a total of sixteen cords.

8. Alternate the cords (see Essential Terminology) and tie four half knots.

9. Repeat step 8 for five more rows being careful not to pull the cords too tight as you work around the circle design.

10. On each of the cords directly beside each half knot, attach a 1.2m (4ft) length of 5mm (³⁄₁₆in) natural cotton rope using a reverse lark's head knot (mounting in total eight cords to give you a total of thirty-two cords).

11. Take two of the just attached cords and two cords from the half knot and tie a square knot.

12. Repeat step 11 around the circle a further seven times to give a total of eight square knots.

13. Remove your work from the project board and lay the macramé on a flat surface. Take your set-aside 35cm (13¾in) wrapped ring and place it on top of your macramé so that the design is centred within it. The wrapped ring now becomes the holding cord.

14. Under each square knot, bring the four cords out straight and mount each onto the wrapped ring using a double reverse lark's head knot, allowing for a space of approx. 10cm (4in) from the square knot to the ring. Note: it is best to mount your first four cords at the top halfway mark of the ring and then mount your next four cords in line at the bottom halfway mark, so that the distance between the macramé and the ring is equal at both ends. Ensure the cord groups are evenly spaced at approx. 6cm (2⅜in) around the ring. This creates a negative space that will be used as the warp for your weave in steps 19–22.

15. Tie a firm square knot as close to the ring as possible, to group the cords together

16. Your ring is now clearly divided into eight sections. Working on the bottom five sections only, fill them by mounting six 1m (3¼ft) lengths of 5mm (³⁄₁₆in) cotton rope in each section (using a reverse lark's head knot), starting with coloured rope and using natural rope in alternating sections. Fill any gaps by mounting extra pieces of the relevant cord where needed.

17. Working on the top three sections, trim cords 1cm (³⁄₈in) from each square knot and tuck behind the back of the dream catcher.

18. Weave in ends, trim cords and fray if desired.

Weaving Element

19. Take the 5.5m (18ft) length of 5mm (³⁄₁₆in) coloured cotton rope (to be used as your weft thread) and starting directly beneath one of the last row of square knots, begin weaving a tabby weave for approx. six rows or 3.5cm (1³⁄₈in). Note: due to the nature of the design there may be times that you have to weave over when you should be going under or vice versa; this is not a problem and just adds to the rustic character of the design.

20. Take the four 3m (10ft) lengths of 3mm (¹⁄₈in) sisal (to be used as your weft thread) and begin weaving a tabby weave for approx. three rows or 2cm (³⁄₄in). Once a complete row is woven, you will need to weave either over two warp threads or under two so that the second row is sitting in the opposite way to the first row.

21. Take the 2.5m (8¼ft) length of 5mm (³⁄₁₆in) coloured cotton rope (to be used as your weft thread) and begin weaving a tabby weave for approx. two rows or 1cm.

22. The final section is woven using the 3m (10ft) lengths of 5mm (³⁄₁₆in) natural cotton rope as your weft thread, working with one piece of rope at a time. Begin weaving a tabby weave until there is approx. 15cm (6in) of cord left, then take your next 3m (10ft) length and begin weaving again. Continue until all four lengths have been used and you have filled as close to the outer ring as possible.

23. Use a weaving finishing technique to weave in cord ends through the back of the design.

Reimagined Director's Chair

This simple pattern will transform an everyday director's chair into something special. Simply remove the fabric from the chair and follow our instructions to create your own macraweave masterpiece. If the dimensions of your director's chair differs from the one we have used, the pattern can be easily altered and adapted to suit your chair's measurements.

Dimensions of the chair we used:
Width: 55.5cm (1 ³/₄ ft)
Height: 87cm (2 ³/₄ ft)
Length: 56cm (1 ³/₄ ft)

Approx dimensions of material we used:
Top panel: 56 x 20cm (1 ³/₄ x ¹/₂ft)
Seat: 55.5 x 56cm (1 ³/₄ x 1 ³/₄ft)

Materials

- 206m (678ft) of 5mm (³/₁₆in) natural cotton rope
- 38.8m (127ft) of 3mm (⅛in) jute
- 22m (72ft) of 3mm (⅛in) sisal
- Director's chair
- Hot glue gun

Techniques

- Reverse Lark's Head Knot
- Half Knot
- Alternating Half Knot Pattern
- Half Hitch
- Overhand Knot
- Tabby Weave
- Soumak Weave
- Weaving Finishing Technique

Preparation

- Cut 32 x 5m (16½ft) lengths of 5mm (³/₁₆in) cotton rope
- Cut 14 x 2m (6½ft) lengths of 5mm (³/₁₆in) cotton rope
- Cut 2 x 2m (6½ft) lengths of 5mm (³/₁₆in) cotton rope
- Cut 2 x 7m (23ft) lengths of 5mm (³/₁₆in) cotton rope
- Cut 8 x 3.6m (11¾ft) lengths of 3mm (⅛in) jute
- Cut 4 x 2.5m (8¼ft) lengths of 3mm (⅛in) jute
- Cut 4 x 5.5m (18ft) lengths of 3mm (⅛in) sisal

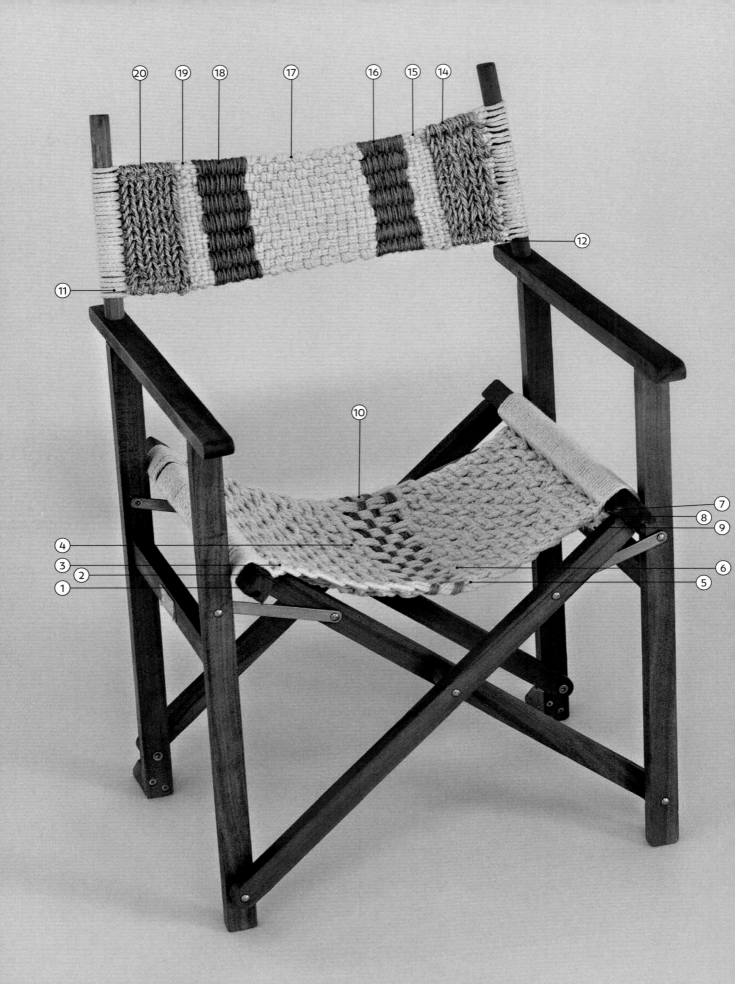

Macramé Element for Chair Seat

1. Starting on the left-hand rail of the chair seat and 3.5cm (1⅜in) from the edge of the rail, mount the thirty-two 5m (16½ft) lengths of 5mm (³⁄₁₆in) cotton rope onto the rail using reverse lark's head knots, working around the vertical poles of the chair legs.

2. Directly beneath, tie a row of eight half knots using four cords as the filler cords and two cords on each side as the working cords, making sure that the half knots are tight up against the chair seat rail.

3. Alternate cords (see Essential Terminology) and tie a row of seven half knots.

4. Continue making the alternating half knot pattern for eleven rows.

5. Drop down 8cm (3⅛in) and tie a row of eight half knots using four cords as the filler cords and two cords on each side as the working cords. This creates negative space 1 that will be used as the warp for your weave in step 10.

6. Repeat steps 3 and 4.

7. Place all cords underneath the right-hand chair seat rail and firmly tie a half hitch knot with each cord around the seat rail, working around the vertical poles of the chair legs. Now turn the chair upside down

8. Starting at one end, take two cords and tie a tight double overhand knot, making sure the knot finishes directly above a half hitch knot. Continue for the remaining cords.

9. Trim cord ends to approx. 1.5cm (⅝in) and push the knots up against the macramé panel so that they are as hidden as possible.

Weaving Element for Chair Seat

10. Using the four 2.5m (8¼ft) lengths of 3mm (⅛in) jute as your weft thread, tabby weave negative space 1 in a four over four under pattern for four rows.

Macramé Element for Chair Back

11. Starting on the left-hand rail of the chair back 2.5cm (1in) above the armrest, mount the fourteen 2m (6½ft) lengths of 5mm (³⁄₁₆in) cotton rope onto the rail using reverse lark's head knots.

12. Number the cords 1 to 28. Bring cord 1 across to loop it around the right-hand rail and tie a firm double overhand knot onto itself, ensuring there is no slack in the cord and that it is straight and level. Repeat with cords 2–28. This creates negative space 2 that will be used as the warp for your weave in steps 14–20. Trim all cord ends to 4cm (1½in), pull them to the back and glue in place.

Weaving Element for Chair Back

13. Turn the chair on its side so the warp cords are vertical and the reverse lark's head knots are at the bottom.

14. Starting from the bottom and using two 5.5m (18ft) lengths of 3mm (⅛in) sisal as your weft thread, soumak weave through negative space 2 in a two over two under pattern for 8cm (3⅛in).

15. Using a 2m (6½ft) length of 5mm (³⁄₁₆in) cotton rope as your weft thread, tabby weave in a one over one under pattern for 3cm (1⅛in).

16. Using four of the 3.6m (11¾ft) lengths of 3mm (⅛in) jute as your weft thread, tabby weave in a four over four under pattern for 6.6cm (2⅝in).

17. Using the two 7m (23ft) lengths of 5mm (³⁄₁₆in) cotton rope as your weft thread, tabby weave in a two over two under pattern for 15cm (6in).

18. Repeat step 16.

19. Repeat step 15.

20. Using two 5.5m (18ft) lengths of 3mm (⅛in) sisal twine as your weft thread, soumak weave through negative space 2 in a two over two under pattern for 8cm (3⅛in).

21. Use a weaving finishing technique to weave in cord ends at the back of the chair seat/chair back designs.

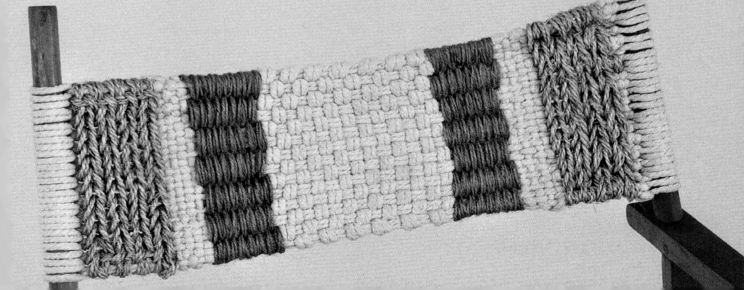

Pride and Joy Wall Hanging

This beautiful wall hanging is a celebration of your mastering of the macraweaving techniques. An explosion of colour and texture, this showstopper will be the talking point of your home and the envy of your crafting buddies. An advanced piece, it will showcase your skills with its wide range of knots and weaving techniques.

Materials

- 41.2m (137ft) of 3mm (⅛in) natural cotton rope
- 144m (480ft) of 4mm (5⁄32in) natural cotton rope
- 5m (16½ft) of 5mm (3⁄16in) natural cotton rope
- 108m (358ft) of 6mm (¼in) natural cotton rope
- 4m (13¼ft) of 10mm (⅜in) natural cotton rope
- 48m (156ft) of 5mm (3⁄16in) colour 1 cotton rope
- 4.5m (15ft) of 10mm (⅜in) colour 2 cotton rope
- 6m (19¾ft) of 5mm (3⁄16in) colour 3 cotton rope
- 4.5m (15ft) of 10mm (⅜in) colour 4 cotton rope
- 12.8m (42½ft) of 5mm (3⁄16in) colour 5 cotton rope
- 32.5m (107¼ft) of 5mm (3⁄16in) colour 6 cotton rope
- 10.5m (34½ft) of 3mm (⅛in) sisal
- 62cm (24in) length of 2.5cm (1in) dowel

Techniques

- Double Reverse Lark's Head Knot
- Half Knot
- Numbering Cords
- Diagonal Double Half Hitch
- Horizontal Double Half Hitch
- Square Knot
- Joining Weaving Cords
- Rya Knots
- Tabby Weave
- Adding Weaving Cords
- Soumak Weave
- Fraying
- Weaving Finishing Technique

Preparation

- Cut 24 x 4m (13¼ft) lengths of 6mm (¼in) natural cotton rope
- Cut 8 x 1.5m (5ft) lengths of 6mm (¼in) natural cotton rope

NEGATIVE SPACE 1: USE LIGHT BLUE/GREY TONE FOR COLOURED ROPE

- Cut 1 x 4m (13¼ft) length of 10mm (⅜in) natural cotton rope
- Cut 1 x 7.5m (24¾ft) length of 5mm (³⁄₁₆in) cotton rope in colour 6
- Cut 208 x 12cm (4¾in) lengths of 5mm (³⁄₁₆in) cotton rope in colour 6
- Cut 4 x 4m (13¼ft) lengths of 3mm (⅛in) natural cotton rope

NEGATIVE SPACE 2: USE PINK/PEACH TONES FOR COLOURED ROPES

- Cut 1 x 4.5m (15ft) length of 10mm (⅜in) cotton rope in colour 4
- Cut 3 x 3.5m (11½ft) lengths of 3mm (⅛in) sisal
- Cut 1 x 4.5m (15ft) length of 5mm (³⁄₁₆in) cotton rope in colour 5
- Cut 69 x 12cm (4¾in) lengths of 5mm (³⁄₁₆in) cotton rope in colour 5

NEGATIVE SPACE 3: USE BROWN/RUST TONES FOR COLOURED ROPES

- Cut 96 x 1.5m (5ft) lengths of 4mm (⁵⁄₃₂in) natural cotton rope
- Cut 2 x 2.5m (8¼ft) lengths of 5mm (³⁄₁₆in) natural cotton rope
- Cut 48 x 1m (3¼ft) lengths of 5mm (³⁄₁₆in) cotton rope in colour 1
- Cut 8 x 90cm (3ft) lengths of 3mm (⅛in) natural cotton rope
- Cut 4 x 4.5m (15ft) lengths of 3mm (⅛in) natural cotton rope
- Cut 1 x 4.5m (15ft) length of 10mm (⅜in) cotton rope in colour 2
- Cut 1 x 6m (19¾ft) length of 5mm (³⁄₁₆in) cotton rope in colour 3

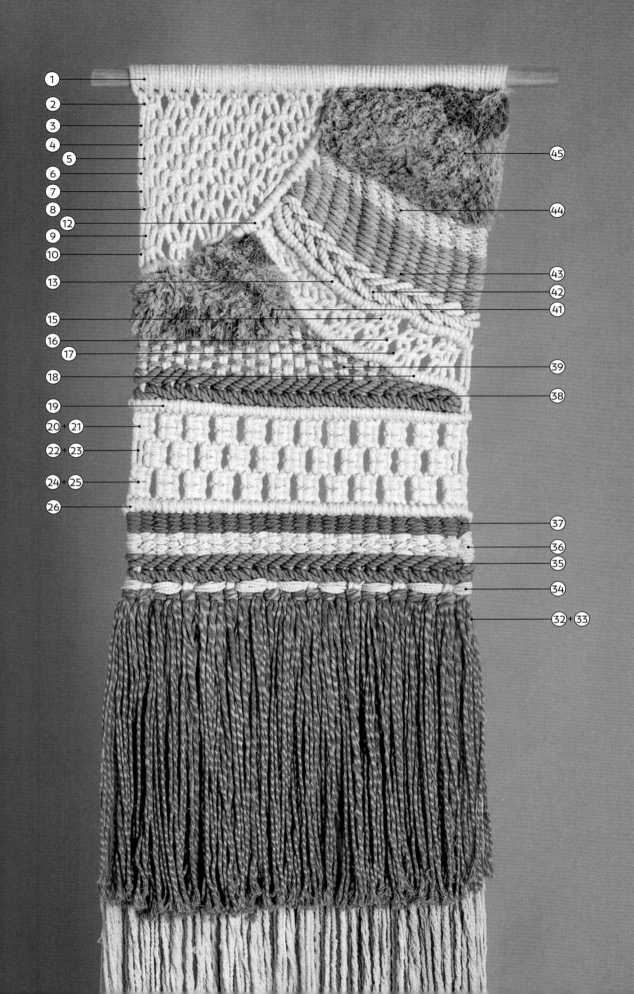

Macramé Element

1. Mount the twenty-four 4m (13¼ft) lengths of 6mm (¼in) natural cotton rope onto the dowel using double reverse lark's head knots.

2. Working from left to right tie a row of seven half knots.

3. Drop down 2cm (¾in), alternate cords (see Essential Terminology) and tie a row of six half knots.

4. Drop down 2cm (¾in), alternate cords and tie a row of six half knots.

5. Drop down 2cm (¾in), alternate cords and tie a row of five half knots.

6. Drop down 2cm (¾in), alternate cords and tie a row of five half knots.

7. Drop down 2cm (¾in), alternate cords and tie a row of five half knots.

8. Drop down 2cm (¾in), alternate cords and tie a row of five half knots.

9. Drop down 2cm (¾in), alternate cords and tie a row of three half knots.

10. Drop down 2cm (¾in), alternate cords and tie a row of three half knots.

11. Number cords 1 to 48.

12. Bring cords 29 and 30 down right to left to border the pattern made by the half knots. These cords together will now become a holding cord (see Essential Terminology). Tie diagonal double half hitches onto the holding cord with cords 1–28.

13. Renumber cords 1 to 48. Bring cords 21 and 22 down left to right. These cords together will now become a holding cord. Tie diagonal double half hitches onto the holding cord with cords 23–48. This creates negative space 1 that will be used as the warp for your weave in steps 41–44. Make sure the largest part of the negative space is 33cm (13in) in length, that is the distance between the double half hitch knot tied with cord 48 and the dowel at the top.

14. Renumber cords 1 to 48.

15. Tie a row of seven half knots, beginning with cords 19–22 and finishing with cords 43–46.

16. Alternate cords and directly beneath (or as close as possible), tie a row of six half knots.

17. Alternate cords and directly beneath (or as close as possible), tie a row of seven half knots.

18. Bring cords 17 and 18 down left to right directly beneath the last row of half knots. These cords together will now become a holding cord. Tie diagonal double half hitches onto the holding cord with cords 19–46.

19. Place two 1.5m (5ft) lengths of 6mm (¼in) natural cotton rope horizontally directly beneath, in line with the last double half hitch tied in step 18 (approx. 43cm (17in) below the dowel. This is now the holding cord. Tie horizontal double half hitches onto the holding cord with all the cords. This creates negative space 2 that will be used as the warp for your weave in steps 38–40.

20. Directly beneath, tie a row of twelve square knots.

21. Directly beneath, tie a row of twelve square knots.

22. Alternate cords and tie a row of eleven square knots.

23. Directly beneath, tie a row of eleven square knots.

24. Alternate cords and tie a row of twelve square knots.

25. Directly beneath tie a row of 12 square knots.

26. Place two 1.5m (5ft) lengths of 6mm (¼in) natural cotton rope horizontally directly beneath the previous row of square knots. This is now the holding cord. Tie horizontal double half hitches onto the holding cord with all cords.

27. Drop down 16cm (6¼in) and place two 1.5m (5ft) lengths of 6mm (¼in) natural cotton rope horizontally. This is now the holding cord. Tie horizontal double half hitches onto the holding cord with all cords. This creates negative space 3 that will be used as the warp for your weave in steps 29–37.

28. Place two 1.5m (5ft) lengths of 6mm (¼in) natural cotton rope horizontally. This is now the holding cord. Tie horizontal double half hitches onto the holding cord with all cords, directly beneath last row of double half hitches.

Weaving Element for Negative Space 3

29. Join together four 1.5m (5ft) lengths of 4mm (5⁄32in) natural cotton rope (to be used as your weft thread). Do this with all ninety-six lengths of the 4mm (5⁄32in) rope, creating twenty-four lengths in total.

30. Working from the base of negative space 3, create a row of rya knots with the twenty-four joined lengths to make the long fringe (see detail photo).

31. Join together the two 2.5m (8¼ft) lengths of 5mm (3⁄16in) natural cotton rope (to be used as your weft thread) and tabby weave for three rows.

32. Join together two 1m (3¼ft) lengths of 5mm (3⁄16in) colour 1 cotton rope (to be used as your weft thread). Do this with all forty-eight lengths of the 5mm (3⁄16in) colour 1 rope, creating twenty-four lengths in total.

33. Create a row of rya knots with the twenty-four joined lengths to make the short fringe.

34. Join together the eight 90cm lengths of 3mm (⅛in) natural cotton rope (to be used as your weft thread) and use to tabby weave one row to the following over (O) under (U) pattern: O2, U2, O4, U2, O4, U2, O4, U2, O4, U2, O4, U2, O4, U2, O4, U2, O2.

35. Using the 4.5m (15ft) length of 10mm (⅜in) colour 2 cotton rope as your weft thread, tie two rows of soumak weave using a two over two under pattern.

36. Join together the four 4.5m (15ft) lengths of 3mm (⅛in) natural cotton rope (to be used as your weft thread) and tabby weave using a two over two under pattern for five rows. Let the cords naturally overlap whilst weaving to create a textured look.

37. Next add the 6m (19¾ft) length of 5mm (³⁄₁₆in) colour 3 cotton rope (to be used as your weft thread) and tabby weave, using a two over two under pattern, for five rows or until negative space 3 is completely woven.

Weaving Element for Negative Space 2

38. Working from the base of the space upwards and using the 4.5m (15ft) length of 10mm (⅜in) colour 4 cotton rope as your weft thread, tie two rows of soumak weave using a two over two under pattern.

39. Join together the three 3.5m (11½ft) lengths of 3mm (⅛in) sisal (to be used as your weft thread) and tabby weave loosely using a two over two under pattern for seven rows.

40. Add the 4.5m (15ft) length of 5mm (³⁄₁₆in) colour 5 cotton rope (to be used as your weft thread) and tabby weave using a two over two under pattern for eleven rows (see detail photo).

41. Using the sixty-nine 12cm (4¾in) lengths of 5mm (³⁄₁₆in) colour 5 cotton rope as your weft thread, create rows of rya knots alternating warp cords with each row to completely fill the remaining area of negative space 2.

Weaving Element for Negative Space 1

42. Working from the base of the space upwards and using the 4m (13¼ft) length of 10mm (⅜in) natural cotton rope as your weft thread, tie two rows of soumak weave along the curved edge using a two over two under pattern.

43. Add the 7.5m (24¾ft) length of 5mm (³⁄₁₆in) colour 6 cotton rope (to be used as your weft thread) and tabby weave using a two over two under pattern for ten rows.

44. Join together four 4m (13¼ft) lengths of 3mm (⅛in) natural cotton rope (to be used as your weft thread) and tabby weave using a two over two under pattern for five rows letting the cords naturally overlap whilst weaving to create a textured look.

45. Using the 208 12cm (4¾in) lengths of 5mm (³⁄₁₆in) colour 6 cotton rope as your weft thread, create rows of rya knots alternating warp cords with each row to completely fill the remaining area of negative space 1.

Finishing the Wall Hanging

46. Fray the ends of the rope on the long and short fringes and trim if desired.

47. Use a weaving finishing technique to weave in all the ends.

30

40

About the Authors

Australian fibre artists Amy Mullins and Marnia Ryan-Raison are back at it again, combining two of their favourite techniques, macramé and weaving, to produce their second book, *Macraweave*. These two friends have been working together in their thriving business Eden Eve since 2015, selling and hiring their macramé and teaching their skills. These macramé maestros have built a loyal following, educating and inspiring like-minded creatives all around the world.

In 2017, Amy and Marnia published their highly successful first book, *Macramé for Beginners and Beyond*. Now they are very excited to present their second book *Macraweave*, an exciting fusion of macramé and weaving. With this modern interpretation, their aim is to add colour, function and beauty to homes everywhere while teaching others how to achieve their dreams as fibre artists.

www.edeneve.com.au

Index

A DAVID AND CHARLES BOOK
© David and Charles, Ltd 2020

David and Charles is an imprint of David and
Charles, Ltd
Suite A, Tourism House, Pynes Hill, Exeter,
EX2 5WS

A catalogue record for this book is available
from the British Library.

ISBN-13: 9781446308059 paperback
ISBN-13: 9781446379554 EPUB
ISBN-13: 9781446379547 PDF

This book has been printed on paper from
approved suppliers and made from pulp
from sustainable sources.

Printed in the UK by Buxton Press for:
David and Charles, Ltd
Suite A, Tourism House, Pynes Hill, Exeter,
EX2 5WS

10 9 8 7 6 5 4 3 2

Content Director: Ame Verso
Senior Commissioning Editor: Sarah Callard
Managing Editor: Jeni Hennah
Project Editor: Cheryl Brown
Design Manager: Anna Wade
Designer: Emma Teagle
Illustrator: Kuo Kang Chen
Photographer: Simone Ainsworth
Production Manager: Beverley Richardson

David and Charles publishes high-quality
books on a wide range of subjects. For more
information visit: www.davidandcharles.com.

Share your makes with us on social media
using #dandcbooks and follow us on
Facebook and Instagram by searching
for @dandcbooks.

Layout of the digital edition of this book may
vary depending on reader hardware and
display settings.